PRAISE FOR *THE RESURGENT CHURCH*

Every leader who is longing to lead in the liminal times we live in would be well-advised to carry a copy of *The Resurgent Church* in his or her back pocket as a navigational roadmap to the future. Drawing from history, biography, technology, theology and wisdom as a global practitioner, Mike McDaniel gives a real gift to the church and those who want to understand the times we live in and how we can move forward.

ERIC SWANSON
LEADERSHIP NETWORK
CO-AUTHOR OF *THE EXTERNALLY FOCUSED
CHURCH* AND *TO TRANSFORM A CITY*

As the cultural ground has shifted under the feet of the church, how does one get a read on where things are and how churches should respond? *The Resurgent Church* helps you exegete the culture and then understand how a church can effectively fit into that moving world long term. It calls for and shows a scripturally rooted way for a lived-out commitment that is a reflection of the gospel. There is much in this book to ponder, both conceptually and practically. I commend it to those seeking a compass to find their churches' way in a changed world.

DARRELL L. BOCK
EXECUTIVE DIRECTOR FOR CULTURAL ENGAGEMENT,
HOWARD G. HENDRICKS CENTER FOR CHRISTIAN
LEADERSHIP AND CULTURAL ENGAGEMENT

Bolstered by solid statistical analysis and laced with insightful missional thinking, in *The Resurgent Church* Mike reminds us of the massively changed cultural context in which we are called to faithfully deliver the message of the church and gives us some insightful clues on how to adjust. This is a really well-articulated book by an unusually perceptive church leader.

ALAN HIRSCH, AUTHOR & ACTIVIST
WWW.ALANHIRSCH.ORG

It's all here: a detailed analysis of the church's current situation, a helpful explanation of the missional-incarnational paradigm, and a practical description of seven essential shifts the church needs to make to find its mission in a post-Christendom age. And it's all written by a warmhearted missionary-pastor who lives what he teaches. Read it. You'll be glad you did.

MICHAEL FROST
AUTHOR OF *THE SHAPING OF THINGS TO COME*,
EXILES, AND *THE ROAD TO MISSIONAL*

Like the CrossFit workouts he does, Mike McDaniel puts us through a rigorous workout of various disciplines all designed to equip the church to navigate this new world. In *The Resurgent Church* he puts us through the traces of biblical exegesis, theological commentary, cultural exegesis, and practical examples of ministry—all in order to prepare us for the rigors of leading a relevant and vibrant church. This volume not only gives hope, but dispenses massive doses of practical suggestions for those who take seriously the role of leading a movement.

REGGIE MCNEAL
AUTHOR OF *MISSIONAL RENAISSANCE*
AND *KINGDOM COME*

The ResUrgent Church

The ResUrgent Church

7 CRITICAL PATHWAYS TO HELP YOUR CHURCH THRIVE IN A POST-CHRISTENDOM WORLD

MIKE MCDANIEL
WITH ROB SUGGS

THOMAS NELSON
Since 1798

Published in Nashville, Tennessee, by Thomas Nelson. Thomas Nelson is a registered trademark of HarperCollins Christian Publishing.

Thomas Nelson titles may be purchased in bulk for educational, business, fundraising, or sales promotional use. For information, please e-mail SpecialMarkets@ThomasNelson.com.

Unless otherwise indicated, all Scripture quotations are from The Holy Bible, THE ENGLISH STANDARD VERSION. © 2001 by Crossway, a division of Good News Publishers. Used by permission. All rights reserved.

Scripture quotations designated NLT are from the Holy Bible, New Living Translation © 1996, 2004, 2007. Used by permission of Tyndale House Publishers, Inc., Carol Stream, Illinois 60188. All rights reserved.

Quotations designated KJV are from the KING JAMES VERSION.

Quotations designated MSG are from The Message © by Eugene H. Peterson, 1993, 1994, 1995, 1996. Used by permission of NavPress Publishing Group.

Quotations designated PHILLIPS are from J. B. Phillips: The New Testament in Modern English, Revised Edition. Copyright © J. B. Phillips 1958, 1960, 1972. Used by permission of Macmillan Publishing Co., Inc.

Library of Congress Control Number: 2016932946

ISBN: 978-0718-0787-7-5 (Softcover)
ISBN: 978-0718-0788-3-6 (e-book)

Printed in the United States of America

16 17 18 19 20 RRD 6 5 4 3 2 1

To my wife, who said, "Don't quit!"
To my children, who said, "We believe in you."
To my mother, who said, "I am proud of you."
To my in-laws, who said, "We've got you covered."
To Grace Point Church, who said, "Take the time."
Plus a special shout-out to Dan Stradtman,
who helped me plow through the data when
I was about to drown, and to Rob Suggs,
who took my academic research and helped
make it far more palatable and digestible.

About Leadership ✳ Network

Leadership Network fosters innovation movements that activate the church to greater impact. We help shape the conversations and practices of pacesetter churches in North America and around the world. The Leadership Network mindset identifies church leaders with forward-thinking ideas—and helps them to catalyze those ideas resulting in movements that shape the church.

Together with HarperCollins Christian Publishing, the biggest name in Christian books, the NEXT imprint of Leadership Network moves ideas to implementation for leaders to take their ideas to form, substance, and reality. Placed in the hands of other church leaders, that reality begins spreading from one leader to the next . . . and to the next . . . and to the next, where that idea begins to flourish into a full-grown movement that creates a real, tangible impact in the world around it.

NEXT: A Leadership Network Resource
committed to helping you grow your next idea.

NEXT
LEADERSHIP NETWORK

leadnet.org/NEXT

CONTENTS

CONTENTS

FOREWORD

Mike has skillfully written an in-depth analysis of the mission challenges facing Western churches as they are nudged to the sidelines in many Western cultural settings. *The Resurgent Church* is written in a popular style, which makes his insights accessible to a wider readership. He explains and cuts through the technical jargon festooning much of the literature dealing with culture and the church's responses. While popular in style it does not oversimplify the complex array of these challenges. His breakdown of the *unchurched,* into the *previously churched* and *never churched* is particularly helpful. He avoids the blueprint, just-do-it-my-way approach by emphasizing the need for each church to prayerfully build its own strategy arising out of its unique context, and by providing a range of resources available online.

The fact that Mike McDaniel and his wife previously lived with their young family in an African village should not escape our attention. Those who have been impacted by such cross-cultural experiences pioneer much of the missional and incarnational ministry undertaken by church leaders today in Western churches. They return, seeing their own culture in a different light and bringing their insights and training to bear as they recognize the missional challenges facing churches throughout the Western world.

Eddie Gibbs
Professor Emeritus of Church Growth
School of Intercultural Studies
Fuller Theological Seminary

INTRODUCTION

I KEELED OVER, FACE FORWARD, DRAWING ONE FINAL BREATH AS THE rubber mat hurried up toward my nose.

Well, maybe that was a little overdramatic. I was going to live. I was even going to do this again. Still, as I crawled across the gym floor with my muscles twisted in knots that would challenge a grizzled old seadog, I thought, *Man, that was awesome!*

Is that a dude thing or what? CrossFit workouts do a number on me. After I complete the workout of the day (WOD), I feel nearly dead and fully alive. And sometimes I catch sight of myself in pools of sweat. Wild hair. Beet-red complexion. I'm going to get a few looks of pity. Some coach will ask me if I have a grandchild waiting to drive me back to the Sunny Acres home.

Nothing like that happened on this particular day. Instead, Alex happened.

I was rolling out my aching, tired glutes and moaning dolefully when he walked up. "I'm kind of atheist when it comes to Jesus," he said, "but I'm willing to talk about him."

That's how it all started—a conversation still in progress.

Alex and I had been friends for about three years. Workout buddies, basically. It was just casual guy talk for a good while, if we talked at all. Exercise and muscle groups and maybe the weather. Then, slowly but surely, we began to catch glimpses into each other's lives.

Alex had grown up in a Catholic home and attended a Catholic school. Religion was part of the curriculum, a program his parents and church, as he saw it, were inflicting on him. And nothing about it seemed authentic.

At that crucial age of twelve, there was a tragic event in his life, something he didn't like to discuss, and he left the school. As he saw it, that meant leaving the church as well. He planned on never setting foot in a church again, and for thirty years he kept that resolution. He cruised through all the rites of passage—adolescence, young adulthood, and seeking the "high life" by experimenting with all kinds of highs. By the time I met him, he had no plans on coming down.

We talked about all this. Mostly I did a whole lot of listening.

At some point, Alex and I began doing our workout of the day together and then adjourning to a local pub for chicken wings. I'll have you know I'm an honorary member of the After-WOD Chuggers' Club, though my chugging was pretty much limited to H_2O.* Over a few wings, our conversations spanned a lot of time and topics. His spiritual beliefs, by this time, were fair game for discussion.

Our friendship is solid, safe enough that we can take out, turn around, and examine more fragile subjects. Alex is sorting it all out: life, God, the church, and what it all means for him at this stage of his life.

I pastor a church called Grace Point, and it was born for the Alexes of the world. Because there are millions more just like him.

---

* I'M NOT A PROHIBITIONIST. I COME FROM A LONG LINE OF ALCOHOLICS, AND EARLY IN LIFE I WAS WARNED BY OUR FAMILY PHYSICIAN THAT I'D HAVE A PROCLIVITY TOWARD ALCOHOLISM. I TRIED IT AND NEVER ACQUIRED THE TASTE. SO I SAVE MONEY AND POTENTIALLY LIVES BY ABSTAINING.

Each Alex has a different story, a different life, and a different winding road that leads to God's kingdom. It's up to us to patiently help them find those roads and make their way safely down them until they reach the safe haven they never knew they craved.

At Grace Point, we say we're a church "for those who have given up on church, but haven't given up on God." Yet we have to face the fact that there are also those like Alex who have given up on church *and* God. As a matter of fact, his tribe is growing far more rapidly than the God-and-church tribe. In a Western world once rich in faith and mission, "no belief" is the hottest religious status of the day. In 2014, the Pew Research Center reported that "no affiliation"—identification with no religious tradition—was the fastest-growing designation among people polled. Evangelicals, mainline Christians, and Catholics all declined in percentage from 2007 to 2014, but those who considered themselves unaffiliated spiked from 16.1 to 22.8 percent.[1]

If our buildings and facilities represented what was really happening, the picture along Main Street would look like this: churches shutting their doors or closing up wings once filled with children and programs, and a fairly new building for the First Unaffiliated Chapel, scrambling to find parking and erect new edifices. But we're seeing it. Old churches are shutting their doors because they're out of ideas, out of time. The great mass of unaffiliateds have no building projects, but they're on golf courses, at the lake, having brunch at restaurants that now open on Sunday, or just sleeping late.

People look at the church as Alex did for most of his life, questioning what it has to offer them and why it even exists. If we had taken snapshots of recent decades, we'd see them like this:

- 1990s USA: 30 percent unchurched
- 2000s USA: 33 percent unchurched
- 2010s USA: 43 percent unchurched

Of the present 43 percent unchurched, 33 percent is dechurched, that is, formerly affiliated but no more. Only 10 percent is purely unchurched with no background in any church.[2] What will the numbers be in another ten years?

I'm not trying to drain your hope the way a good workout drains my strength. As a matter of fact, it's just the reverse. If we look beyond the unsettling trends, we begin to see something entirely encouraging. Churches are reinventing themselves and finding ways to survive, flourish, and break through to Alex and those like him in these new times.

I spent some time studying a number of these churches with the questions, What do they have in common? What are they doing to defy the trend of their times?

There's plenty of disparity in these churches. Each has its own personality and mind-set. Personally, I advocate a diversity of expression. Yet there are common themes we see in these breakthrough congregations. They understand their times, their communities, and their mission. They've also learned how to unpack for a new generation what is eternal and unchanging in the biblical church—and also what unhelpful baggage to leave behind.

I tried not to come away with a momentary portrait of these churches but to look at them over a five-year period in order to see how they managed transition and how they've sustained their community impact. My hope is not that I'll provide new templates for copycat startups but that church leaders will recognize and commit to the principles that are worthy and effective.

There is so much we need to learn, so much we can't delay doing. On the other hand, there is so much renewed passion and exhilaration in rediscovering how to be the church Jesus always wanted us to be and how to reach an Alex, knowing how Jesus loves Alex and how much Alex will love Jesus if we can get the two of them together.

As in all times of upheaval, there is stress and delight in equal measure. It's all in how you choose to approach it.

Alex and I have eaten our fair share of wings. He's had a few glasses of beer over a few months, and we've forged a friendship that I now have grounds for hope will be an eternal one. My friend has found his way tentatively back into church but with an open mind.

As a matter of fact, the other day he asked me if I would buy him a Bible. He'd grown curious about those pages he assumed were dry and irrelevant. Alex is on a path, and you and I know where it leads. The destination makes all that we do—all our momentary frustration and heartache—more than worthwhile, because it reminds us that God is still in charge.

The old church doors no longer swung open in Alex's direction. He had turned on his heel at the age of twelve and walked away. To get him to come back, we needed something new and relevant to someone like him. It couldn't look much like that old doorway, but on the other hand it had to lead to the right place and on the right terms.

This book is about building and managing those gateways into a future that God has ordained you and me to enter, like pilgrims entering a promised land.

PART ONE

THE KINGDOM IN EXILE

THIS WAS ONCE CALLED CHRISTIAN CIVILIZATION. THE WORD *Christendom* began to appear in the earliest forms of the English language. Only around 1400 CE did it come to take on the meaning of lands dominated by the Christian religion.

Current histories tell us that Christendom's potent ruling force in the Western world extended to the early modern era. In the age currently described as "postmodern," the faith described in the Christian Bible no longer dictates cultural or political directions.

For some time, most church leaders lived in denial of their fading prominence in the world. In our times, however, the truth can no longer be overlooked: the church is on the outside looking in. An accustomed earthly kingdom awakened to find itself in exile.

How did it happen? What are the new realities of post-Christendom? And what should we be doing now?

ONE

UNINVITED

Who Changed the Rules?

IT'S THANKSGIVING IN A TYPICAL AMERICAN HOME.

There's furious scrambling in the kitchen as the cooks prepare to unleash their arts. The house carries the best aroma of the year. When the news comes that dinner is served, even Uncle Alan is willing to turn off the football game without a quarrel.

The family circles up in the living room. Grandfather delivers one of his famous ornate blessings, every head bowed, every eye closed, every mouth watering, and every soul wishing he'd hurry up.

The word *amen* is like an opening gun. *They're off!* Everyone accelerates toward the great table to claim a strategic place. There are two tables, of course. The big table is finely set in the dining room. It has leaves that fold out for such occasions, enabling most of the family to pull up a chair.

Most.

"Aw, Mom, do I have to sit at the *children's* table again? I'm not a kid!"

Yes, there's also a children's table, usually in the kitchen.

As seats are assigned, the family sorts itself out. Elder and important members eat in the dining room. They discuss the big events of the year.

3

Then there's that other table—the one for kids and cousins, Sis's boyfriend, and, you know, the family's spare parts. Some claim it's more fun at the kids' table, but let's be real—these are the Thanksgiving cheap seats.

Why do I paint this picture? Because something similar has come to pass on the American cultural scene. If you're a church person, you've noticed it just as I have.

Christianity no longer has a seat at the big table. It's the oddest thing, isn't it, because they've folded out all the leaves there—more diversity in the conversation than ever and nearly all voices are welcome.

But Christianity has been shunted aside. It's now the family's aging great uncle, a relic of the past who (they say) isn't quite as sharp lately. He can sit with the kids and the grab bag of the so-called others.

Yet once he was a true patriarch. When he gave the blessing, everyone listened. He sat near the head of the table, sometimes even carved the bird, and his opinion meant something.

I hear whispers about all this in our culture. The great uncle still has his fans, and they believe he still has something to say, still believe he deserves a voice.

But what's to be done? The rules have changed.

How did we get here?

WELCOME TO POST-CHRISTENDOM

We know exactly when Great Uncle Christianity got his seat at the main table.

In 313 CE, Constantine was the emperor of a declining Roman Empire. He announced his personal conversion to Christianity and then issued a decree that this young religion would be tolerated.

His sincerity has always been questioned. What we know is that he was a master of political timing.

Christianity was no longer a minor religious fad. The emperor's own mother was part of the movement. Most of all, Constantine understood the common goals of church and state, and so, for the first time, Christian leadership was welcomed to the great table. Christianity and culture were deeply intertwined for better or for worse.

From this moment on, Western culture was influenced and then wholly shaped by a biblical worldview. When Rome fell, the faith still stood. During ten centuries of medieval disunity, the church preserved education and encouraged the arts. Throughout Europe, local cathedrals were the very center of town life. People went there to learn, to receive medical assistance, and to maintain community. God was the sole subject of the arts, from architecture to painting to sculpture to stained glass.

Even when the Renaissance was marked by an awakening of learning and exploration, it was accompanied by reformations that brought vitality to religious faith, both in Catholicism and the new Protestantism. As explorers ventured across the seas, they sought to export God as much as to import gold.

With the rise of science, technology, and new philosophies, the church began to hear competing voices for the first time in ages. Even now it offered the dominant perspective, the true north of the cultural landscape. But the cognitive dissonance between faith and reason in Western culture could only increase. To some there was an obligation to choose one path or the other. Were we fallen and sinful, as the church taught, or were we neurotic and ill, as medicine and science diagnosed our situation? Was the universe the work of a Creator or of the laws of physics? Were the laws of ancient Scripture still binding, or should they be rewritten by each succeeding generation?

In modern times there was also the rise of the global village. Advances in communication and transportation brought out the voices of other religious faiths—or of no religious faith. Old assurances that God (*our* God) was in his heaven and all was right with the world no longer seemed so certain. The very grounds of common assumption in nearly every subject began to shift. Since time immemorial, everyone had known who made the rules and what they were. Now it was clear there was an old, fading system and a new, ambiguous one.

The old system had been known as Christendom. Within it, public conversation had been guided by New Testament faith and its spokesmen. Art had been understood as being for the glory of God. Education, often provided by the church, molded Christian citizens. Commerce was regulated by a biblical ethos. And cities and governments were designed by men and women steeped in Christian thought.

This doesn't mean, of course, that the world was synonymous with the kingdom of God, only that the church, whatever quality it happened to maintain, had a place of authority in Western culture. Kings and presidents made sure to quote the Bible when they made decrees, no matter how biblically questionable those decrees might have been.

One would have thought Christendom represented a true and satisfying saturation of the gospel. Yet anyone who reads history closely knows that what we called Christendom was largely a hollow frame of institutions, a Christian facade hiding an empty soul.

As a result of this cultural mesh, the church made a subtle but sure move to becoming an institutional model rather than a movement of countercultural force and impact. The kingdom of God became confused with the kingdoms of the world.

The new and more diverse system can be described as post-

Christendom. This is the world we've come to know, a world in which many competing voices vie for the hearts and minds of the community. It's been coming along for decades, and we've responded in various ways. For a time there was resentful talk of moral majorities opposing cultural elites, but the plain truth must now be faced: Christianity can no longer lay claim to any dominance within the population.

Numbers and percentages aside, we could also say that the Constantines of today—in government and in our culture at large—no longer find this faith to be a necessary tool for them in reaching their goals. They recognize that the world is far more complex and multilayered, and they rule (or write or film or schedule Sunday soccer practices) accordingly. We are left to reminisce about the good old days or perhaps to be more intentional, to be proactive rather than reactive.

LIKE A THIEF IN THE NIGHT

This is not a post-*Christian* culture but a post-*Christendom* one. That is to say, the church has great numbers and a voice (or several alternate voices), but other conversations drown us out.

It's important to keep these two terms sorted, otherwise our dialogue becomes confused. Many people use *post-Christian* when they mean *post-Christendom*. Why is the distinction important?

One has theological ramifications while the other has ecclesiological ones. A post-Christian world would be one where Christ and his church have no future. Christianity would be dead. Once we begin to speak of such a thing, we've given up hope. We've quit long before the race is over.

In our postmodern world, however, we know that spirituality is alive and quite vibrant in all its many forms. People are searching for a connection to God just as they always have. It's part of our belief system, of course, that we're actually wired this way, so the idea of a postspiritual human being is an impossible concept.

Even so, people are looking for their connection in places other than traditional church settings. We'll see examples of more creative churches sprinkled across the landscape, identifying with and understanding their culture of subculture and creating thoroughly biblical environments that speak to the postmodern heart. And there's nothing post-Christian about that.

When we say post-Christendom, we're talking about the relationship of the church to the world in which the power structures of the two are entwined together. Within a generation or two, we've seen a shift away from that reality. Things began to change before any of us were born, but it has been perceptible throughout our lives. Most of us can point to times when things were different, no doubt more harmonious with our personal Christian values. Now we look around and comment with a tinge of nostalgia: "This trend would have been frowned upon" and "Good discipline was a part of every home but is now a lost art."

Until very recently the changes have been discussed as if they were something ominous and in the distance, not an imminent threat. But objects in the rearview mirror turned out to be closer than they appeared. Real change is no longer at our doorstep; it's come in through the window and is now remodeling the house. You see it in the redefinition of the ancient, long accepted practice of marriage. What could be more basic to Christianity, to any religion, to humanity itself than one man plus one woman? With the lightning success of the LGBT movement, the effect of post-Christendom has become chillingly clear.

The new standards (or lack of them) came like a thief in the night, and suddenly we perceive ourselves to be on the outside looking in. We can't put a finger on the moment of reversal, but suddenly we are the ones being marginalized, and it's not a comfortable feeling.

As a simple measurement of the shift, our parents often heard the Bible read by a teacher every morning in elementary school. Prayer and the pledge began the day. Yet the Supreme Court evicted the Bible, and in 1986 the United States graduated the first public school class whose education never included the Bible within its curricula. This brings us to a time when George Barna tells us that only 3 percent of the nation's thirteen-year-olds have a biblical worldview.[1] Have we become the moral minority?

At least four markers demonstrate the decline of Christendom in our time.

MARKER ONE: CHURCH ATTENDANCE HAS DECREASED

Near and dear to every pastor's heart is the full-house index. The numbers once held a comfortingly predictable rhythm. In the summertime, pews emptied out a bit. But sure as the leaves changed color in autumn, the people came, celebrated Christmas and then Easter in large numbers, and then dispersed again to the beach or the lake. If growth stagnated, at least there was a steadiness provided by the generation that built our economy from the 1950s onward.

Under Christendom, people simply attended church—by law, by peer pressure, or by choice. Businessmen knew it was good business to sit on church committees. Politicians flaunted their churchgoing credentials.

In post-Christendom, faith lives while Sunday attendance is an option. Part of it is a generational phenomenon. The steady builder-gen class is rapidly vanishing. Generations X and Y (birthdates 1966–94) make up 34 million of the 58 million who don't attend church weekly.[2] It's difficult to get accurate figures concerning how many North Americans attend church due to the reliability of those being questioned. But one of the more careful surveys, compiling data from more than 300,000 Christian congregations, concluded that less than 18 percent of the population regularly attended church.[3] Another author cited the *World Christian Encyclopedia*, which claimed that 111 million Christians were churchless as of 2001.[4]

Again, these are not post-Christian times, but one of the meanings of post-Christendom is that people no longer feel the authority of the church in guaranteeing their participation. Church attendance, as everyone paying attention knows, has been declining for decades. And now we have a generation of younger Americans who have never known what it means to be a regular, involved part of a church fellowship.

Far fewer people are having their lives changed through the active body of Christ. If they practice Christianity at all, they believe they can practice it outside the doors of the traditional church. We need to wake up to the fact that the citizens of post-Christendom don't share our assumptions that we have what they need or even—if they do share our beliefs—that we're the sole distributor of what they need.

NO-CHURCH NATION

As of 2014 when the estimated number of unchurched adults in the United States stood at 114 million. Add to that the roughly 42 million children and teenagers who are unchurched, and we have 156 million residents who aren't engaged with a Christian church.

To put that in context, if all those unchurched people were a separate nation, it would be the eighth most populous country in the world, trailing only China, India, Indonesia, Brazil, Pakistan, Bangladesh, and the remaining churched public of the United States (159 million).[5]

MARKER TWO: CHURCH EXISTENCE HAS DECREASED

Doors are closing. Have we considered the repercussions of that?

In a post-Christendom world, hostility toward the established church has grown. Traditional churches have a low public approval rating, and that has contributed toward many of them struggling to keep their doors open. There are fewer churches per capita in America than in the past. In 1900 there were 27 American churches for every 10,000 people. By 1950 there were only 17 for those 10,000. And by 1996 there were only 11.[6]

AMERICAN CHURCH TO PEOPLE RATIO		
1900	1950	1996
27:10,000	17:10,000	11:10,000

But don't we read about exciting new churches starting up all the time? Yes, we do. As a matter of fact, 4,000 churches are born in a year when 3,700 die.[7] That's a relative stability that fails to account for total population growth. There are more people, more people groups, younger people, and too few of them within range or interest of the startup churches.

American Christianity is in serious decline, measured by the shrinkage of its franchise operations in relation to the customer base. Scholars believe that, just as religion once shifted its operation from the Eastern to the Western Hemisphere, it now shifts just as surely from the North to the South. The heart of our work once moved to Europe, then to North America, and now to Latin America, Africa, and points of Asia. Will the last vibrant Christian to leave the United States please turn out the lights—or so say the cynics.

MARKER THREE: LOOSE SPIRITUALITY HAS REPLACED STRUCTURED CHRISTIANITY

Post-Christendom also doesn't mean postspiritual.

By all accounts, spirituality is blossoming. But the quest has moved from a social and authoritarian one to an inner, free-spirited one. People explore every option, and traditional ideas of received truth no longer register in any special way. The question has become, "What works for me right now?"

Spirituality, as defined in Christendom, was a life attainable exclusively through a local church. Free thinkers, as they were called a century or more ago, were looked upon with suspicion. Post-Christendom opens up the possibilities, and the result is that spirituality itself is less threatening for being more customizable. Institutionalized Christianity is seen more and more as an outmoded path, one with baggage, old-fashioned preconceptions, and a lack of free expression.

The churches are emptying. Denominations are cutting their staffs. Christian principles are systematically giving way to new value systems. And yet, all the while, people are telling pollsters that they pray daily, that they believe in heaven, and that they do indeed think there is a God. They are simply brewing their own home recipes rather than buying the old brand-name stuff.

MARKER FOUR: THE MARGIN OF SEPARATION BETWEEN CHURCH AND STATE HAS INCREASED

The United States came into being at a time when the relationship between church and state was in crisis. Christendom had reached its peak, and its days were already numbered.

When separation of church and state was written into the heart of American law, a line was drawn for the first time in Western culture. In the past, kings had carried the presumptive endorsement of heaven. Just as David and Solomon had been priestly kings, heads of government continued the tradition into the age of reason—but no farther. In the United States, government was to establish no religion, and churches had no political power. Churches enjoyed their newfound freedom, but they were less eager to give up their traditional hold on public policy. As long as church and state functioned among the same population, this was bound to be a difficult issue.

Such episodes as the 1925 Scopes Trial over the teaching of evolution captured the turf battle between the two forces. In a democratic environment, the people were left to work out these issues through public debate and, ultimately, the ballot box. A more recent battleground was the Supreme Court battle that ensued when Alabama judge Roy Moore fought the forced removal of the Ten Commandments from a government building. For many observers it was easy to see the symbolism as the carvings of the Mosaic law were stripped from the walls of an American courthouse. Later would come the debates over Christmas manger scenes on government property. A few decades earlier, no one would have questioned the biblical imagery. Prayers were offered before college football games. Church ministers maintained close relationships with the public schools. And usually there were no problems. But those were the waning days of Christendom.

In our time, those who resented closing their eyes for the public prayers or who opposed the words *In God We Trust* on our money understood that they were faint voices of minority dissent. Who was going to listen? Now those voices have found strength in numbers. They aren't hesitant to point out those places where they feel organized religion has overstepped its bounds.

And the bounds seem to grow more and more restrictive by the day. Pastors worry about how much longer they can receive zoning approval for new buildings, for extended parking. And is the day coming when churches will lose their tax-free status? Just a few years ago it would have been unthinkable. Now one can't be sure.

The uneasy feeling of recent decades finally has a name: post-Christendom. And it's no longer a theoretical threat, no longer fodder for disapproving sermon illustrations. It's here.

The question we face is, "How will we respond?" Could we be headed for a second Reformation? The one in the sixteenth century was based on orthodoxy, that is, it was built on the question, "What are the right beliefs?" The new Reformation would be built around ortho*praxy*, meaning the question of right practice. "How shall we then live?"

How indeed? If you're a medical doctor, it's quite important to have all the right knowledge. But you'd better know the correct way to practice it in the operating room. As today's churches approach the patient that is contemporary humanity, where do we make our incisions? What are the right tools?

---------------- TWO ----------------

UNDECIDED

Where Do We Go from Here?

I HAVE FRIENDS WHO WORK IN THE WEDDING FIELD. FOR THE PURPOSE of this book, I'll call them Kevin and Leslie Green.

One day Leslie met a caterer who was interested in bringing the Greens some clients who wanted to be married. The caterer pulled out her pad and began asking questions about the Greens and their policies for weddings and receptions. Leslie gave her all the information she could think of and added, "E-mail me and I'll send you the pricing details."

As she and the caterer were preparing to go their separate ways, the caterer dropped in one more detail. "By the way," she smiled, "this will be a same-sex marriage. I'm assuming that's okay?" This took Leslie off guard, and the caterer quickly added, "Listen, if it's not all right, I'll respect that. I mean, you have to do what you think is right."

For Leslie, this issue had simply never come up. When she and her husband became wedding planners, she never thought of a moment like this occurring. Like most people, she had been raised with a mental image of what a marriage was, and that image always showed one man and one woman.

Leslie formed her words carefully, sensitively, as the caterer had done. She didn't gasp, flare up, or make self-righteous comments, as Christians are often predicted to do in the media in such situations. She said, "I would like to think about that a little bit. I really appreciate your understanding that this is a new thing in our business. Let's talk again about this."

The Greens tell me they're definitely not comfortable with same-sex weddings and receptions. On the other hand, they see their work as a ministry, and they don't want to cut themselves off from new relationships. There are other issues too—legal issues. In the current political climate and following recent Supreme Court rulings, is there even a decision to make? This particular caterer was courteous, but what if another client wanted to press the issue? Same-sex marriage is now legal in all fifty states.

They consulted a lawyer, and he said: "You can choose with whom you want to do business. But you also have to realize there are always repercussions. You can end up with TV news trucks outside; you can bear the brunt of whispering around the neighborhood by those who will depict you as closed-minded and fundamentalist and homophobic; and, yes, you could be paying me to defend you in a lawsuit."

As I write the Greens aren't certain what they're going to do. They're praying and thinking. Aren't we all?

Transcending the same-sex angle, weddings are a lightning rod in ways we couldn't have imagined a few decades ago. Church settings for ceremonies are quickly becoming a thing of the past. In Australia 70 percent of weddings are now conducted civilly, according to the Australian Bureau of Statistics.[1] Among Catholics in the United States, church weddings dropped by 40 percent between 2000 and 2012, according to the Official Catholic Directory.[2] Post-Christendom shows in the secularization of country, and never is that more clear than in the cultural foundation of families.

The problem is underlined when some young couples come to

the church to request a ceremony. Quite often they like the visuals: the architecture, the backdrops for wedding photography, the tradition-drenched ambience. But when the pastor mentions marriage counseling, sparks fly. When the spirituality of the service and of the wedding itself are brought up, the couple becomes angry. They didn't come for religion; they just want to be married!

Does the pastor compromise his standards so as not to lose his opportunity to build a relationship with this couple, or does he insist on church policies and chase them into a civil ceremony?

Marriage represents one of the central battlegrounds—perhaps *the* central battleground—in the church's fight for relevance in the cultural conversation. Is marriage a unique Christian institution, or is faith an optional accessory? Should the pastor perform ceremonies for nonbelievers? Gay or lesbian couples? Interfaith couples (Protestant/Jewish or Mormon/Evangelical)?

In this and many other issues, church leaders have the terrible feeling of standing on shifting sand. Where do we go from here?

The key to understanding our plight is in grasping the big picture.

In the past, when such questions arose, we would step back, take a look at the church, and ask, "How can we do this better?" If attendance was declining maybe we just need better attendance, prompted by new programs and an exciting new sermon series. Or maybe we need to move the church to a different neighborhood. Or find some new leaders. In other words just do the old dance a little faster, put on a better show.

This thinking doesn't solve the problem, because it fails to address the great changes that have come to pass in the world around us. Our identity has changed not because we're failing to perform our old tasks well enough but because the modern landscape has shifted. The questions we ask should go deeper. New questions must touch theological, anthropological, and philosophical issues at the heart of people and society.

The world of this decade is simply not the same place, and seismic quakes have moved the church from the center to the fringes. The world no longer hears the voices of pastors as having any special authority. Instead, pastors speak for one organization among many. They might say, "You shouldn't be holding these soccer practices on Sunday," and people ask, "Why should your opinion count any more than the soccer coach's?"

The first time we hear it, we are offended. The second, we're angry. And at some point we may begin to panic. Where do we stand? What are the rules now that "the Bible tells me so" no longer carries the same currency in public discussions?

Some, of course, gear up for war. They issue battle cries against the winds of changes, calling for the restoration of the Christian values on which our country was built. Somehow, it is believed, we can pass enough laws or organize enough boycotts to get this country back to its Bible-believing ways. And if the world is recast as the enemy, at some point we need to ask who is left to evangelize.

Others simply raise the white flag of surrender, though they might not characterize it as such. They look at a frightening new cityscape, then at the comforts of churchianity, and say: "We call this room a sanctuary for a reason. This is my rock, my hiding place."

In short, these people decide they like it at the children's table. So the big table doesn't want us? Who wants to sit with people like that anyway? We have more fun at the little table. Just let us pour more money into the church campus, erect a new family life center, and schedule enough activities so we can walk away from the degraded world once and for all. If you can't beat 'em, abandon 'em, because we can redecorate the rooms in our parallel universe and make it all cozy. We have *us*. And if anyone wants to be evangelized, they know where to find us.

The only problem with that outlook is, of course, that Jesus won't sign off on it. No matter whether we read the Gospels sideways, upside down, or inside out, we can't imagine Jesus with a retreat strategy. He believes in advancing and engaging.

We have to face the fact that Jesus still cares about the conversation at the big table, whatever the subject may be. Not because he loves conversation, but because he loves the people who are doing the talking. So we need to bear in mind that when we run away from the world, we're running away from Jesus, who never will.

STUCK IN THE MIDDLE WITH YOU

Alan Roxburgh of the Missional Network bought us a word out of sociology and anthropology: *liminality*. It may be unfamiliar but it's worth understanding. Those who study other societies, particularly tribal communities, speak of *in-betweenness*. A young warrior goes through a ritual and finds midway that he is no longer the man he was and not yet the warrior he is to become. He feels disoriented. Victor Turner first studied liminality in the behavior of African tribes, and his observations have carried over into groups and situations of all kinds, including the plight of the modern church.

The Latin *limen* means "threshold," the bottom of the doorway that is neither in nor out. Roxburgh, in a short study of Turner's work in Africa, applied the concept to the church's contemporary crisis. My family saw this firsthand in 1998 when we lived and worked with a tribal group in Zambia. They had certain rites of passage that had to be navigated. Likewise the church finds itself between two worlds but is a citizen of neither. Yet this is the identity of the church when it properly understands itself as caught between the kingdom of God and the kingdoms of this earth.

None of which makes our plight any easier. Roxburgh focused on the feeling that we've suddenly become invisible to the larger society.[3] The church is simply waking up to the fact that it has been a modern institution in a postmodern world and that something's got to give. Inevitably, since Jesus speaks to every human condition, he speaks also to this new one. It is our task to follow the steps of Jesus into a postmodern world and to observe how he moves, teaches, and heals in this community.

Yet another leader in the missional movement, Alan Hirsch, underlined the fact that while all things are made new in the world, nothing is truly new in our basic task. This "in-between place," he argued, is actually our permanent address, for the church was never meant to set down hard roots. It's healthy for the church to live in constant transition.[4]

After all, the New Testament paints a picture of a church in constant flux and even constant crisis. There is always a tension between the Word and the world. This idea of permanent change may be a bit unsettling to comfort-loving people, but Hirsch was undeniably on the right track. Change is the leading indicator of life. Only death is static. Jesus, who never had a place to lay his head, was constantly on the move, constantly engaging his society, and he calls his followers to the same life.

As we think about enlisting for the culture wars, we need to realize that, in the words of *Star Trek: The Next Generation*, resistance is futile. Fighting inevitable change is a barrier to our creative engagement in the newness around us. Chaos is always the seedbed of creativity. In the Old Testament, the voices of the prophets rose in profusion when Israel and Judah were on the edge of new and frightening worlds. It seemed to the people that God suddenly had a lot to say.

Yet when does he not? We've all heard the quip, "Just when I thought I knew all the answers, they changed the questions." In these times in which everything is up for discussion, the church has an opportunity to take its shot at the new questions, because whatever they are, the answers themselves are still the same.

We're seeing the first creative expressions of the church's response to the new questions. These expressions themselves will remain fluid. We hear phrases and ideas such as "emerging," "emergent," "fresh expressions," "future," "ancient-future," "house," "organic," "gospel-centric," and "missional," and we find we need a special dictionary just to keep up with the conversation. For many years pastors avoided the term *postmodern* itself, seeing it as a concept from philosophy, having nothing to do with what transpired within church walls. Now we need to grasp the difference between emergent and emerging and understand why ancient-future is more than a cute oxymoron. To capture these terms is to hold a momentary snapshot of how the church, or parts of it, are beginning to engage a post-Christendom world.

There are many nuances to the glossary above, their meanings and histories and concerns. Some insist on keeping things simple (or simplistic) by herding all of them into the one lightning-rod term *emerging*, because that one can be seen as a movement with identifiable faces. Fair or not, we can apply a one-size-fits-all label. But the church's recent responses to new cultural realities are much richer and more complex. Most of us need to read more, watch more closely, and have a far more detailed understanding of what is going on around us. Just as Luther, Calvin, Henry VIII, and Loyola made important distinctions while sharing the status as movers and shakers of the Reformation, today's people and movements cannot be crowded together into a simple all-purpose idea.

BACK TO EGYPT?

We also need to ask ourselves what our fear or panic says about our theology. Do we truly believe that after twenty centuries the good news is old news? Do we believe the people God created have finally gotten themselves completely beyond his reach? Has society digressed so far to the left morally that the right people can no longer touch them?

Anyone who thinks so may not have read the fine print in the New Testament when they answered God's call. Jesus promised to go with us to the ends of the earth. He said that all authority in heaven and on earth is granted to us through him. Our gospel is built to last.

While we're answering that question, we might need to look in the mirror and see if an Israelite from the wilderness period is staring back. When the followers of Moses were wandering in the wilderness, they wanted to turn back to Egypt. They may have been slaves there, but at least they had three square meals per day and a place to sleep. Things weren't perfect, but everyone knew what was what. There's a trace of this thinking in those who yearn for the 1950s, when everyone sang the same hymns their parents and grandparents had sung, and when nobody was offended by their newfangled television's public service announcement to "go to the church of your choice this Sunday."

Do we really want to go back to Egypt? Because there's something to be said for manna from heaven, for God leading with a pillar of clouds by day and fire by night. We all know it's the times of uncertainty in life we ultimately remember most fondly—the early days of marriage and adulthood, the days when we have to scramble, the in-between times. The early church was at its best when it was young and unsteady on its feet. It has consistently been a victim of its own success yet a victor in persecution.

The wilderness period of today may be uncomfortable, but it's also thrilling. Even as we hear so many voices of lamentation, we hear others whispering with excitement, "Something is happening—what will God do next?"

Leonard Sweet, professor, author, and visionary, likes what he sees. Where others speak of this present darkness, he sees the ingredients of a new spiritual awakening and claims it will be led from outside the church.[5] With the title of one book, he urges Christians to *Carpe Mañana!* Seize tomorrow!

Sometimes it's a simple decision to see the proverbial glass as half-empty or half-full. For example someone could point out the severe decline in Great Britain's church attendance that has been going on for decades.[6] Yet he could just as well point to exciting pockets of spiritual awakening that are being noted in the same place.[7]

What we can all agree on is that the center no longer holds. We were there once, but now, in fact, there is no center at all. We want to claim that something like secular humanism is a ruling voice, but the truth is there are no ruling voices in the postmodern world. One of the chief complaints against organized religion is its claim to the existence of absolutes, and absolutes don't fit well into a smorgasbord of worldviews.

We need to embrace hope. Christ can rule from the center of people's hearts without ruling from the center of their public square. As a matter of fact, he did his greatest miracles from the fringes. Should we be upset if the signs point to him doing it again?

In some European countries religious taxes have been levied against anyone enrolled in the church, whether Catholic or Protestant. Not surprisingly the church was seen only as another financial entanglement, not to mention one that seemed to provide little in exchange. In Germany it has been estimated that committed Christians make up no more than 3 to 4 percent of the population.[8] This nation, the heart of the Protestant Reformation, has what Jesus would call fields white with harvest. The question is, can these people be better reached from the center, where there are large, empty cathedrals and birth taxes, or from the fringes, where there is freedom to respond to the momentary and heartfelt needs of people? What if the church learns to present itself as coming to give rather than take? What if we learn to articulate the true freedom we experience rather than offer the impression of a burden of rules and regulations?

Some Christian leaders have realized that if Jesus has been pushed to the margins, then he is where he is most comfortable. Standing before Pontius Pilate, he had little to say. But among the masses, the marginalized, he had plenty to say and to do.

Or are we too much like the people of his time who wanted him to be a king? Who wanted him to fight his way past the soldiers, avoid the cross, and make his way to Rome? The first one to suggest that scenario suggested it to Jesus in the desert, along with two other ideas that Jesus also rejected. Jesus chose the harder road, and it's hard to imagine he doesn't have a plan for us to walk it with him now.

Let's get comfortable on the edge of society. Let's find a way to look at our confused surroundings and see them as the place Jesus once found, finds now, and will *always* find as his most profitable place of ministry.

So may we find the same.

PROFILE: EDDIE GIBBS

Dr. Eddie Gibbs is Senior professor emeritus of church growth at Fuller Theological Seminary and a leading figure in conversations about the church and its future.

Q: Dr. Gibbs, why do we use the word *post-Christendom*? Isn't post-Christian a simpler term?

A: When we say post-Christian, we're speaking of the weakening fruits of the church. It's a term that is directed to our failures of mission. Post-Christendom, on the other hand, is about the collapse of a geopolitical system or worldview. It's a big-picture view of the world at large. You can be Christian in a post-Christendom world, of course.

Q: What are the implications of the difference between these two ideas?

A: We live in post-Christendom. That's a fact, and we don't get to vote on it. Our decision is whether we are going to be post-Christian or not. That's a question of what we do and how we live.

Q: We find ourselves in a situation much more similar to that of the early church. What can we learn from them?

A: I would use this comparison. In post-Christendom, we must coexist with sexual sin within the very framework of society—but so did the first Christian generation in a "pre-Christendom" world. In Roman culture, pederasty—homosexual acts between men and young boys—was open and tolerated. The church had to recognize it was surrounded by a world that lived under a different moral code.

Q: What difference did this make for the early church, and what difference does it make for us?

A: The church had to own a clear grasp of what its mission was and what it was not. It was not to push through large-scale changes of the culture but to let the gospel change individuals. Then, of course, from individual transformation, the work of Christ would make "all things new," ultimately in culture as well. Above the door of our church, we keep a banner that reads: "Come as you are. Don't leave as you came." That places the emphasis where it needs to be—on Christ meeting us where we are, then changing us from the inside out.

Under the influence of Christendom, ecclesiology became separated from missiology, to their mutual impoverishment. The urgent task now facing the churches in the West is to develop a reconnected ecclesiology and missiology and to demonstrate what a missional ecclesiology will look like within Western contexts.[9]

THREE

UNEXPECTED

Jesus on the Edge

IT'S HARD TO DO, BUT IT'S A USEFUL EXERCISE. IMAGINE YOU'VE NEVER heard of Jesus. You've been brought up without a single detail of his story ever being mentioned. How would you respond to it?

My family moved to southern Zambia in 1997, and we lived for four years among the Tonga people. Most of these folks are farmers who live week to week on whatever they can grow. We fell in love with our village, and we shared our lives with the people and learned to see the world through the lens of their culture. To this day I'm still close to friends in this village.

Our children played with Tonga children, with toys no more sophisticated than soccer balls made of trash bags and cars crafted from old milk cartons. Like all children, they used their imagination to create worlds, and they got along wonderfully.

One of the tools we used for evangelism and discipleship was the *Jesus* film. Once we had established a new church, we would play the film to deepen faith in Christ. Also, it was a wonderful tool for reaching out to villagers we hadn't met.

You've probably read about the *Jesus* film and its adventures across the world. It's a straightforward cinematic account of Luke's gospel and was filmed in 1979. Those who distribute the film have translated it into hundreds of languages. It's been viewed not only in places where Jesus was unknown but sometimes where *movies* were unknown. We were excited to have it available in the Tonga language to help them visualize the life and work of the Master.

I'll never forget the first time we had a showing of *Jesus*. It was a big event with the novelty of a motion picture projected onto a screen. Everyone in the village arrived in the afternoon. For hours the people sat patiently, waiting to see this show that seemed like magic.

When the sun finally disappeared behind the trees, I looked at the great crowd—children sitting together on the ground, the women clustered together, and the men scattered on mats or leaning against trees. Even the local witch doctor attended, as curious as anyone else, but standing at a respectful distance.

We fired up the generator, and the hum of quiet conversation ceased. People made gentle exclamations as the bright picture appeared—a window into another world. They saw the hills of Judea and heard a narrator addressing them in their own tongue. The pictures on the white screen came to life. People walked and talked, and one marvel after another played out before their enraptured eyes.

I would use the word *awe* to describe the crowd reaction. But the greatest emotional response by far came when Jesus began to speak. For some reason, it was wonderful and shocking that he, Jesus, should speak Tonga. We had been told by the nationals that Jesus was a white man's God. Yet he used the words of the village! That the disciples, the crowds, the Romans, and the religious leaders would speak their language was no surprising matter. But Jesus!

We had told them in many ways that Jesus was also the God of the Tonga people, but hearing his words with their own ears settled the question once and for all. After the film, a woman said to me: "This is an amazing thing! I never knew Jesus spoke our tongue!"

We left Zambia in 2001, but to this day there are thriving New Testament churches in the Zambezi valley, where that film was shown, because Jesus is the God who speaks their language.

I wonder if people today realize that Jesus speaks their language. We've certainly tried to get that message across. But what would it take for people to see Jesus in the flesh as one of their own?

I submit to you that in this regard the differences between our culture and that of the Tonga people is diminishing quickly. People in the West may be much more comfortable with technology, but they're just as certain that Jesus is somebody else's God. If he isn't the God of some other nation, then he's just the God of some other time. He doesn't speak to a time that includes terrorism, the Internet, Ebola, same-sex marriage, and pharmaceutical solutions to every need.

It's a new reality, for we've become accustomed, over hundreds of years, to Mainstream Jesus—the Jesus who is welcome at city hall, in the courtroom, and at the best parties in town. We serve a Jesus whose political views, we suspect, are very close to our own. He may love all nations, but he has a special place in his heart for the good old US of A.

Jesus may have made a few statements about rich versus poor, but he would wink at us and say that American-style prosperity is a great thing as long as we remember to tithe. Most of all, we serve a Jesus whom all our friends also serve. Jesus is the most popular guy in town. Even when we watch football, the players stop and point to heaven after touchdowns as if to say, "You the man!"

Mainstream Jesus has been an easy sell for a long time. Quite often he was either the only game in town or close to it. There's not too much about him that was marginal.

Which is why we need to see him through other eyes occasionally. If we have friends, coworkers, and even family members who seem to have harsh, negative views of him, we probably need to find out just how they see him and why. How could growing numbers of Westerners see Jesus so differently and so angrily when people in Zambia and other such places fall in love with him at first sight?

There is only one Jesus, but there are countless perceptions of him—and there always have been. Jesus asked Peter, "Who do people say that the Son of Man is?" And then he asked Peter, "But who do you say that I am?" (Matt. 16:13–15). Both questions need to be asked. The people watching the film had an advantage because they knew nothing at all about the man in the film. They had the advantage of first impression. But in the Western world that's almost never the case. People have already made up their minds about Jesus.

So Jesus comes to us and asks us first what we're hearing about him around the neighborhood. Then he asks us, "What about you? What do you think?" The fact is that our view may need just as much recalibrating as everyone else's.

I believe a fresh look at Jesus within his time and his world will help us understand who he is in our time and in our world.

IN ON THE GROUND FLOOR

What I'm about to relate is a version of what we call gospel, that is, the good news. None of this information is likely to be new to you, but don't skip over it. We need to revisit the basics of the story as frequently and as freshly as possible. We can't afford to let it become old news. This is a time when we once again need a strong reminder of just what it means for the God of all creation to be poured into flesh.

Incarnation means "taking on flesh." This word, never actually used in the Bible, is nonetheless the foundation of every word, thought, and idea in the New Testament. There is gospel because there is incarnation. There is hope for every person on the face of the earth because of incarnation. Internet blogger Michael Spencer pointed out: "Without the incarnation, Christianity isn't even a very good story, and most sadly, it means nothing. 'Be nice to one another' is not a message that can give my life meaning, assure me of love beyond brokenness, and break open the dark doors of death with the key of hope."[1]

Suffering in our humanity, we could become nothing better. We were incapable of becoming gods, so God became one of us. That changed everything. Whatever issue in life confronts us, the solution always arises from the concept of God in flesh. It's true of this present crisis faced by the church. Again we need to look to Jesus and find our way.

What does the incarnation have to do with this moment in time?

Perhaps the essential presentation of the idea is found in Philippians 2:6–7, where we learn Jesus Christ, "though he was in the form of God, did not count equality with God a thing to be grasped, but emptied himself, by taking the form of a servant, being born in the likeness of men." Paul used the word *kenosis*, which means "to empty," here. The Bible we used for centuries, the King James Version, told us instead that Jesus "made himself of no reputation," but that doesn't capture the concept at all. No, the more precise meaning is that God *emptied* himself into flesh. Though he was God, he took the form of a man.

Professor Millard Erickson wrote, "The magnitude of what he gave up is beyond our power to imagine, for we have never seen what heaven is like."[2]

The author of Hebrews called Jesus "the radiance of the glory of God and the exact imprint of his nature" (Heb. 1:3).

Paul told us elsewhere, "For in him the whole fullness of deity dwells bodily" (Col. 2:9).

John said, "The Word became flesh and dwelt among us" (John 1:14).

Each time the New Testament expresses this idea, it uses new words and images because there is no one way to say such a thing definitively. It defies common thought. There simply aren't words in any language that can capture the power of the concept of God pouring himself into flesh. But we must find the words, and I'm partial to the Philippians approach: he *emptied himself*—poured himself into flesh—and not in the shape of a king but of a servant.

Jesus chose to work from the margins of humanity, to get in on the ground floor and work up. So there are two key ideas with which we must reckon: first, that God would become one of us, and second, that he would become one of the *lowliest* of us.

When we understand his mission, it makes complete sense. A mission is a rescue operation, and it always requires risk and sacrifice. To go out and find what is lost is to put oneself in harm's way, and how would it have served for God to come and take the job of King Herod or the Roman emperor? He wasn't interested in redeeming the world from the top down through better government. The whole counsel of history, which he could view at once from his eternal throne, showed the impossibility of that.

In the person of Jesus, God set forth to rescue and redeem his children starting from the very bottom.

As we study the nature of Jesus, we're led to two strong conclusions:

1. His very nature and mission were incarnational. He reached people by going among them.
2. He provided people the model for us in continuing his work. "As the Father has sent me, even so I am sending you" (John 20:21).

It follows that if he reached people by going among them, so should we. Our lives and ministries should identify as closely as possible to the language and life of the people and culture in which we find ourselves.

As a matter of fact, effective Christian leaders have done this throughout history. E. Stanley Jones, the missionary and friend of Mohandas Gandhi, established meditation chapels for Hindus, encouraging them to come and meditate on God's Word. He gave them a name from their own culture—ashrams—but they were repurposed as vehicles for God's Word. Jones understood that Hinduism and culture were tightly intertwined. Indians in America who came to Christ had to give up everything else about their cultural origins. Jones wanted Indians to be able to bring Jesus back into their own culture.

This is not a new or trendy concept, just one long past due for rediscovery. It's time for pastors and leaders to come out from behind their desks, walk through their office suites, and reenter the world. They need to be deeply involved in their communities, not tokenly involved.

In the past we've seen church leaders urge their members to bring their friends to church, yet they've struggled to create a model of that. They've had to admit they have few if any nonbelieving friends. The church culture is too comprehensive, too consuming.

On Friend Day they've desperately offered invitations to Joe the auto mechanic who seems like a nice guy or Bob, who is on the team repaving the church parking lot, whom they never really knew before today.

"Participants in the inviting community will seek to draw others to Christ by embodying that gospel," the late Stanley Grenz pointed out.[4] Embodiment is the operative concept. To embody the gospel is to live out the gospel in the darkest avenues and deprived places so that our actions give credibility to our words when we speak the gospel.

The really scary thing is that the most dedicated members don't have too many nonbelieving friends either. How can they get around in the world if they're always at church?

It's a recipe for a dying church, a post-Christendom church.

Mission arises at the margins rather than at the center.

—PAUL PIERSON[5]

RADICAL RENUNCIATION

God chose to be manifest in Jesus in a particular culture at a particular time, and his arrival was a clear message about the kind of mission he intended. He chose an obscure peasant girl as a mother, and not only did he choose a downtrodden nation as his home but Nazareth—a village not even mentioned in the Old Testament, the Apocrypha, by Josephus, or in the Talmud—as his hometown. People from Nazareth were ridiculed. And though sages from the East came seeking the newborn king, only a band of lowly shepherds was sought to share the moment. Never could there have been a less royal birth.

From the beginning he understood the road he must take. At the outset of his ministry, he faced three temptations in the wilderness. In each, the choice was how to use power—to feed himself supernaturally, to win glory by casting himself from the pinnacle of the temple, and to take hold of the world by making a pact with the devil. In short, bread, circuses, and politics. He rejected these shortcuts and chose the way God was showing him. He would take hold of the world all right, but by winning hearts rather than seizing power. He renounced the way of the world, which is force. His power comes through sacrificial love, not coercion.

Thus he spent his time, not with the movers and the shakers, but with the poor and the desperate. He had time for everyone who requested it, healing and helping wherever he went. So difficult was this message that it constantly eluded the disciples' grasp. Acting as bodyguards and hurrying him through crowds, they pushed children aside. Yet Jesus stopped and cared for those children. They, of course, were the most marginal people of all.

He touched lepers who were accustomed only to being cursed and kept at a distance. He gave dignity to fallen women, known sinners, and the general dregs of society. What puzzled the religious leaders most about him was his refusal to distinguish the sacred from the secular. Those leaders dressed and presented themselves as special editions of humanity and heavenly ambassadors of rules and regulations. Jesus saw everyone as a child of God. He taught that rules were in the service of people and not the other way around.

He built no tabernacles. He established no mission headquarters. But he was on mission at every moment. His mission was people, wherever and whatever they were. He started with people where they were rather than where he wanted them to be.

When he taught he painted a picture of a kingdom that appeared to be a photographic negative of the world's kingdoms. He said that those who would be the greatest must learn to serve, that the first would be last. He brought good news to the poor in spirit, to those who mourn, to the meek, and to the persecuted. He addressed those who were on the margins of society and told them this was their time. As Dietrich Bonhoeffer put it,

God is not ashamed of the lowliness of human beings. God marches right in. He chooses people as his instruments and performs his wonders where one would least expect them. God is near to lowliness; he loves the lost, the neglected, the unseemly, the excluded, the weak and broken.[6]

He hadn't come simply to speak in the abstract about such a kingdom; he came to demonstrate how it worked. And the most shocking part was that the way it worked was to get him crucified. He took the side of the marginalized until he took their fate as well. And so ended, it appeared, the great experiment of trying to stand conventional wisdom on its head.

But we know the rest of the story. What seemed like an ending was really a beginning. New life could come through surrender to death. The God-man had exchanged his perfection for our corruption so that we could be redeemed. As Jesus stood before his disciples in his resurrection glory, they saw the fulfillment of his teachings: the last had become first, the suffering servant had become the ruler of all.

It didn't happen despite his working from the margins—it happened because of it. To understand that truth is to grasp our future hope.

THERE GOES THE NEIGHBORHOOD

Five times the Greek word *skenoo* ("dwell") occurs in the New Testament, always from the apostle John's pen in either his gospel or the book of Revelation. It means to pitch one's tent in a place and live among its people. It's yet another image of Incarnation—God pitched his tent and came to be one of our tribe.

> And the Word became flesh and dwelt among us, and we have seen his glory, glory as of the only Son from the Father, full of grace and truth. (John 1:14)

You don't pitch a tent only to install plumbing and electricity and maintain your own comfortable ways. If you've come this far, you go native. In his paraphrase *The Message,* Eugene Peterson captures this image by saying God "became flesh and blood, and moved into the neighborhood."

We would call that a missionary presence, though we're very slow to learn. It's intriguing that Paul earned his way as a tentmaker in the city of Corinth (Acts 18:3) even though Greeks despised manual labor and even though he carried the status of apostle. He pitched his tent among the people he visited and even helped sew the tent.

After Paul's journeys and the early growth of the church, the success of Christendom actually slowed down any movement in world missions. Only in 1780 did a poor shoemaker named William Carey begin to push the idea of intentional foreign missions. Ironically, as the church has slowly lost political power, it has stepped up its outreach to the world, finally pursuing the task Jesus set out in his Great Commission.

Yet now the paradigm of taking the gospel to the world is being turned inside out. In post-Christendom we must retrain our minds. Christians of other nations are beginning to arrive on our shores, just as we once sent missionaries to China or the Philippines. During these times, as we find ourselves again on the cultural fringes, we must begin to think as missionaries of our own neighborhoods. Thankfully, the book of Acts carries the blueprint for us.

In Acts 2 we discover how the church can work from the margins of society.

> And day by day, attending the temple together and breaking bread in their homes, they received their food with glad and generous hearts, praising God and having favor with all the people. And the Lord added to their number day by day those who were being saved. (vv. 46–47)

Like Jesus they focused on people and relationships. They simply lived out their faith in public, showing a model of joy and love in the simple acts of living—taking meals and going to the temple. And we're told repeatedly they leaned on the power of the Holy Spirit, who trumps any marketing plan or program strategy.

We can also see that God was with them. Even then he was working to bring the most vicious of their persecutors, Saul of Tarsus, into their fold as the most brilliant of their leaders. Do we believe God is with us? Can we have faith that he is going to perform the out-of-left-field miracles he's always done when his people trusted him?

Acts is a simultaneously miraculous and realistic book. Every page underlines the tension of believers on the edge, contending with hostile Hebrews, incredulous Romans, and people of the many cities who have never heard the first fact about Jesus. How were the first Christians so successful? Yes, the Holy Spirit had come in triumph, and the disciples trusted and relied upon him. But could it also be that the good news is mightiest when it is truly news?

The *Jesus* film was shown to a rapturous audience who received it as if it were happening for the first time at that moment and in their presence.

Can we learn to share the gospel with such immediacy?

Can we trust the Holy Spirit to prepare the hearts of people who crave redemption?

Can we learn the cultural language well enough to talk about Jesus within its vocabulary?

Can we come out from among the church programs and hot bands and cool campuses to personally engage people in the community, where we can't rely upon ecclesiastical trappings—no matter how timely—and rely only on the power of the Holy Spirit, missionary-style?

Can we weave our theology together with a missiology into the fabric of our lives?

Younger leaders are giving us hope by doing this very thing.

Many of them are becoming bivocational ministers not by necessity but by choice. Starbucks barista seems to be a popular choice for meeting people and building relationships in the newest version of the public square. Josh Kelley's coffee-serving experiences inspired his book *Radically Normal*.[7]

He commented that so many of today's Christian books are calling on believers to be radical—and that's a good thing. But we also need to be normal. He cited the example of the Iced Tea Lady, a loud, Jesus-praising Christian whose voice could be heard across the room. When she looked in the mirror, she saw someone who was expressing the joy of the Lord. But did she ever look from the perspective of the others in that room? Do they see the difference that Christ makes—or do they just see *different*?

Through experiences such as these, Kelley came to see not only the world from the inside out but the church from the outside in, and he began to learn things they can't teach you at seminary.

For a long time we've been good at critiquing our culture, but not so good at *exegeting* it. That means to interpret by reading "out." Instead of examining simply to criticize, we need to examine so as to *understand*. We've been skipping that step. When we exegete our surroundings, we begin to comprehend the underlying reasons for what we've simply branded as unbiblical. Deeper understanding brings us the compassion Jesus had from within his culture. But it also helps us to penetrate and saturate that culture with his gospel.

The ever-present spirit of judgment has created a disconnection between the church and the world, and that division is unnecessary. The day is gone when we can deal with the world by pointing to a Bible verse and expecting people to fall in line. In Christendom, it could work, but this is a new day, a day in which the theme song is no longer "The Bible Tells Me So" but rather "Come, Let Us Reason Together"—accent on the word *together*.

As we reason together, getting to know those who don't bow to scriptural authority, we're looking for answers to why questions. Why has your life brought you to the assumptions you now hold? Why do you feel Christianity has nothing to offer you?

It might just be that, in cartoonist Walt Kelly's words, "We have met the enemy, and he is *us*." It might be the way we've represented ourselves to the world. It may have been our lack of engagement with the needs of the community. It could be any number of things we've done or failed to do in creating unnecessary obstacles to an encounter with Christ.

We like to quote Paul's statement that the gospel is "folly to those who are perishing" (1 Cor. 1:18), but that shouldn't include the extra layers of foolishness we've applied. Paul, like Jesus, penetrated the ideas and practices of the world around him. He peeled away the cultural layers until he came to the heart that is common to all humanity—the naked heart that will hear and respond to the call of the Spirit.

This is why many young church planters are being encouraged to live in their communities for a year or more before doing any official church work. It's a refreshing change, following the lead of the early believers and going instead of waiting for others to come. Like Paul in Athens we stand in the marketplace of ideas and beliefs and bring news of the "unknown god" (Acts 17:23).

Let me suggest that this is an advantage, not an obstacle. It worked for Jesus. It worked for the early church. And it will work for us in a new world for which Jesus still has good news.

PROFILE: JASON'S STORY

At the beginning of the book, I shared the story of a CrossFit friend named Alex. Jason is another friend from my workout world, another wanderer in a dark world of hurt. If we're going to live incarnation-ally, we need to venture into the places where the Alexes and Jasons are waiting for us. I'll let him tell his story.

My mom was fifteen when she brought me into the world—a kid raising a kid. From the beginning, I was exposed to sub-stance abuse, violence, infidelity, and crime. I knew no other experience, so I thought these were everyday parts of life. We were poor.

By the time I was ten, my parents were divorced. I lived with my mother, then my dad (which I didn't want), then Mom again. To be honest, though, I raised myself for the most part. There wasn't a lot of healthy moral direction during my forma-tive years. And when I was sixteen, one of my "stepdads" stuffed a wad of bills in my hand and told me to go hire a prostitute.

The last conversation I ever had with my dad was the day my own child, a beautiful daughter, was born. "You'll be a lousy dad," my father told me before disappearing from my life once and for all. When I was growing up, my world was shades between deep gray and darkest black. I had no way to know the world's spectrum included bright, vibrant colors as well.

I did know I wanted to escape, and college was my only ticket to do that. I worked a couple of jobs at a time to get through, and ultimately I earned a degree in computer science. That's when Walmart made me a job offer as an entry-level programmer. My job was actually the first steady thing in my life; I'm still with Walmart.

Marriage didn't go quite as well. I thought that work and home life would finally give me the joy I desperately needed. But we fought all the time. Even the addition of Jessica, our daugh-ter, couldn't save our marriage. We ended up divorced. At that point, I tried the loose life: wine, parties, women, and ultimately another stab at a real marriage. This one had problems too. We were a blended family, and we fought over how to parent our two daughters.

At CrossFit I met Pastor Mike. We became friends, and as I desperately looked for ways to save my marriage, I found myself taking my wife to church. I hadn't been in a sanctuary since my grandmother died. But Pastor Mike seemed real. We were friends in sweat and aching muscles before we ever talked about spiritual things and marriage issues. We had done a lot of grinding* before we ever started praying. Maybe church could help me. I became a Christ follower.

In 2013 my wife and I became covenant members of the church, and more important, I said yes to Jesus Christ as the ruler of my life. Things were looking up—until my wife left me anyway. My life hit rock bottom.

Winter set in, and I was grieving the loss of my marriage. I remember dragging myself to church one morning, utterly miserable but needing to be around people, needing to see if God was there. Those sitting around me must have thought, "That guy's a mess."

I prayed through the service, went home, and had an emotional breakdown. I cried out to God from the bottom of my hurt, and to my deep comfort and relief, I heard him answer. He gave me a sense that the storm had passed and he would care for me.

I doubled down on two relationships: my daughter and my Lord. One day, in a men's group study of experiencing God, we were studying the way God called Moses. I asked God to show me what I could do for him.

Thirty minutes later I was putting Abby to bed when she

---

*Grinding is CrossFit lingo for working out.

looked up at me and told me she wanted to follow Christ and be baptized. That was exciting enough, I promise you. But then she smiled at me and said, "Daddy, I want *you* to be the one to baptize me."

I was blown away. To me, I heard God saying, *I can use you in ways you've never imagined. There are no limits.* I couldn't contain my deep emotions as we prayed together.

Before a host of friends and family, I baptized my daughter at church in 2015. I was also allowed to tell my story to the church. That day my heart was full.

I've discovered there are a lot of colors in God's rainbow. He rescued me from a world of misery, and he lives in the hearts of my daughter and me. It's also nice to know he had a church willing to reach out and embrace me when I was so lost and wounded. I'll spend the rest of my days being thankful.

FOUR

UNCOMFORTABLE

Farewell to the Easy and Predictable

WHEN IT WAS FOUNDED IN 1902, *POPULAR MECHANICS* WAS ONCE the go-to magazine for modernist thinkers who believed a wonderful new world lay ahead, all made possible through the triumph of science and good, well-oiled machinery. A century or so later, the magazine is still going strong.

Back in the day *PM* readers were keen on visions of the future. A 1950 essay about tomorrow's America, for example, foresaw the proliferation of solar energy—used primarily to power the many farms that would surely continue to define America. Also predicted for the farm (in a 1960 issue) was the proliferation of farmers in high-tech radio towers, guiding their heavy machinery by remote control.

A 1929 issue predicted that future clothing would mostly be fashioned from that wonderful fiber asbestos. In 1935 statistician Roger W. Babson told us, "Within twenty years, more than half the population of the United States will be living in automobile trailers." The trailer trend was big in the midthirties, so surely it would take over the housing industry. Then a colorful 1951 magazine cover showed a man opening his garage to start up his personal helicopter.[1]

The problem with predictions has always been that we see the future through the lens of the present. We figure today's priorities will be just as important tomorrow. We can all plot a line on a graph when we spot a growth area. We just don't expect the line on the graph to swoop, dive, or disappear from the page entirely. The problem with change is that it changes.

Thus a mid-twentieth-century prophet would look across the landscape and assume a farm-based future economy with futuristic tools. He would ask what was next for the railroads or what kinds of souped-up radios families would use for listening to cowboy stories on weeknights in the twenty-first century.

Few anticipated the move to an information-based society or the declines of farms and even factories. And the Internet? As recently as 1995 a columnist in *Newsweek* ridiculed the idea that anyone would ever buy anything online. He wrote, "So how come my local mall does more business in an afternoon than the whole Internet does in a month?"[2]

Nearly two decades later Amazon announced revenue of $89 billion for fiscal 2014—and that's just one Internet company. It isn't just our gadgets that transform the world; it's the world around them and particularly the ideas that define that world.

Anyone in the 1980s anticipating an Internet-driven economy could have made monstrous profits by investing in that idea. Then, if she foresaw the 2007 global financial downturn, she could have cashed out in time and stayed afloat.

What makes the future so elusive is disruptive or discontinuous change. Ordinary, predictable transformation (*incremental* change) is enough of a challenge for most of us. We all know what it's like to see the growth of this or the fading away of that. The great test of our times, however, is that curve ball the future always has in its pitch selection.

And in these times changes have been far more rapid and far

less continuous. This has created a stressful situation for the church. During the last quarter of the preceding century, normal change suddenly began to give way to the disruption of a culture no longer evolving but morphing into something else or, more accurately, into many somethings. Alan Roxburgh argued that we can no longer discuss our culture in terms of a true center. It is now "an organized diversity with little sense of defining center."[3]

Within a culture not only changing but decentralizing, what is the church to do?

THEY CHANGED THE QUESTIONS

I earlier mentioned the adage "Just when I finally had all the answers, they changed the questions."

Indeed, there was a time when ministerial students attended seminary in order to focus on biblical scholarship and took classes to help them understand church structure and ministry philosophy. An effective curriculum would consider the cultural environment of the world and prepare students accordingly. It was a workable system.

During the 1950s American life was steady and prosperous. Families and suburbs grew, and denominational churches did their thing much the same way their parents had, taking into account incremental changes in society but still forging ahead with the same hymns, the same sermon approaches, the same kinds of programs. Churches still held summer tent revivals, pack-the-pew Sundays, and calendared activities throughout the week. Leaders attempted to understand their world, but to some extent they could still set their own agenda, asking for people to organize their lives around church fellowship by serving on committees, investing in building plans, singing in the choir, volunteering in the nursery, or whatever was needed.

Today the church no longer feels confident in setting an agenda for its people. Commitment has shrunk. Seminaries are less certain how to prepare the next generation of church leaders. As the world has piled changes upon changes, the church has had no recourse but to reinvent its structures and rethink its strategies. No longer is the local church at the center of the universe—but nothing else seems to be either.

In 1962 D. James Kennedy founded Evangelism Explosion (EE), one of the most successful church programs of that era. It simply mobilized Christians to go into their communities and share the gospel, often with strikingly fruitful results. The presentation was based on solid curriculum and scripted conversation strategies. This was the era of the Avon lady and college students selling encyclopedias door to door.

In 1997 Kennedy's organization conducted a study of its process and found that its methods were perceived by many as "confrontational evangelism."

Dr. Kennedy didn't necessarily agree, but he addressed the perceptions. Admirably, EE announced it would retool its approach. There would be less emphasis on cold-call encounters and more on the building of relationships (something Dr. Kennedy felt had always been at the heart of his ministry). In-depth discipleship would become a stronger goal.[4]

Campus Crusade for Christ, another product of the mid-last century, also spent time in self-examination. Among other things, the ministry changed its name to Cru. In a global village the word *crusade* had intensely negative connotations, particularly among Muslims whom Cru hoped to reach.

Meanwhile another campus-based Christian ministry, Inter-Varsity Christian Fellowship (IVCF), was rocked in 2014 by banishment from the nineteen campuses in the California State University system. The problem was that IVCF insisted on appointing

Christian students as officers; however, Cal State's newest requirements were that all approved student organizations must be fully inclusive.

In other words refusing to accept a non-Christian in a leadership position disqualified IVCF from recognition as a campus group. Needless to say, emotional arguments ensued across the Internet. But after a year of nonrecognition, IVCF was welcomed back to Cal State's system. The two groups had talked it out and found workable compromises.

These are examples of parachurch ministries rather than the church itself. They tend to be built more like businesses, with the freedom and flexibility to adapt. Rapid adjustment is far more difficult for congregations answering either to governing boards, congregations of members, or denominational hierarchies. Yet adjustments and reinventions, built around the nonnegotiables of the biblical gospel, cannot be avoided if the church is to survive and thrive in a post-Christendom world.

Clearly the church can't be bounding uncritically into the future, blissfully unaware of its surrounding world and the forces that confront it. We need first to understand it if we're going to have any chance of formulating strategies for moving forward, no matter how pure our intentions or how solid our theology. Jesus first commissioned his disciples with these words: "Behold, I am sending you out as sheep in the midst of wolves, so be wise as serpents and innocent as doves" (Matt. 10:16). In its simplest terms that's a call toward ministry that applies mind and heart, with neither trying to overcome the other but being both intelligent and compassionate.

We must begin by using our minds to discern the forces shaping the world. In the balance of this chapter, we'll look at several crucial shifts that have brought discontinuous change in our culture. These cultural shifts, let's remember, are all intertwined. None can be comprehended as if existing in a vacuum.

ECONOMICS: GLOBAL SHIFT

The first prophet of the twenty-first century economy was Thomas L. Friedman with his book *The World Is Flat*.[5] The meaning of his title was that the *playing field* was flat because a global economy created new and more competitive conditions.

Yet Marshall McLuhan first popularized the term *global village* in the early sixties,[6] in reference to the effect of modern telecommunications. But by the time Friedman wrote, the revolution was in process. His book seemed edgy in 2006 upon publication, but it's almost matter-of-fact now, as we've seen so many effects of the globalization he described.

We usually discuss the economy in this trend, but globalization extends far beyond commercial matters. We've moved from a personal life defined by local community to one touched by various elements of a vast world. The implications for cultural merging and diversified community are profound.

Globally directed corporations, for example, will obviously value the idea of diversity because their markets involve many more cultures than they did previously. While it's easy enough to couch this in moral and ethical terms—all people equal before God—the underlying motive sparking this development is economic profit. Whatever the reason, the end result is often a positive one. People have stronger understandings and greater respect for other traditions and beliefs.

Missional Churches see new opportunities in globalism. In other words if the world is shrinking, it's more accessible to us and to the gospel. Mosaic Church in Los Angeles commissioned 150 missionaries to go beyond US borders to the world's most populous cultures and territories. As long as the world is more globally aware, why not make our churches more aware of the mandate of Jesus to go to every corner of the world, teaching and baptizing?

Sociologist Robert Wuthnow has pointed out that mission spending hasn't just increased, it has absolutely surged, even in a time of local financial challenge. Mission funding in local churches has jumped by as much as four billion dollars—an increase of 50 percent over one decade.[7] Surely this is an encouraging development, given the constant initiatives to fulfill the Great Commission by a particular date during the course of most of the twentieth century. It took cultural globalization, not preaching, to help our people finally think in terms of gospel globalization.

Here is evidence of impressive growth in third-world missions during the last third of the twentieth century, not just an increase in mission efforts but mission results.[8] In the third world, churches are opening doors, expanding, and penetrating new cultures.

LOCAL WORSHIP CENTERS		
Location	1970	2000
Africa	282,000	603,000
Latin America	131,000	462,000
Asia	234,000	1,246,000

The most intriguing development of all has been *glocalization*—a word that may lack a musical sound but makes up for it with a robust theology when applied to the Christian scene. For our purposes glocalization means being on mission globally and locally. Doing that requires an understanding of the all-embracing universality of the gospel to all people as well as understanding the particular incarnational appeal to our local neighborhood.

Postmodernism often shows paradoxical sides. For example, big-box stores and niche shops thriving simultaneously. Glocalization is an example of concurrent mega- and micromovements in a comprehensive application of our faith.

We've seen church planting become the latest trend in church growth. It's far from a discouraging development, even with the inevitable, disheartening stories of failed plants. The fact remains that many churches are becoming seasoned and adept at growing the kingdom glocally, with church plants across town as well as across the globe.

SOCIOLOGY: MULTIETHNIC SHIFT

Rudyard Kipling was the most acclaimed author in the late nineteenth century. His poem "The White Man's Burden" coined a phrase that took hold quickly, capturing the idea of Western imperialism being led by one particular race and culture. Kipling and many of his contemporaries believed in a godly mandate, somewhat secularized from the Great Commission, to extend American-European dominance throughout the world.

There were, of course, Christians who made some proper distinctions. When Hudson Taylor brought the earliest Christian missions to inland China, he received tremendous criticism for failing to import English clothing and other trappings along with his faith teaching. He and his party wore Chinese apparel and adopted, as closely as possible, local customs out of respect for the people. But this was considered shocking and demeaning for any Englishman. As most of us know, there were always missionaries who brought Western hymns and insisted on speaking their own languages to those to whom they tried to minister.

We come full circle in the present age with a shift from monoethnic to multiethnic understandings. It seems obvious enough, but the change of mind-set has powerful implications. We've thought of one group as a de facto ruling class, a so-called first world that dominates the second and third worlds. For so many reasons we're prevented from thinking in those terms. Our neighborhoods are far more diverse. We watch television shows and movies that take great pains to show us casts of characters that look like an America that is no longer strictly white and middle class.

As a matter of fact, we enter a period in which race itself is a far more elusive category, given the increase in the number of people who identify themselves as multiracial. Only as late as 2000 did an American census, for the first time, offer respondents the opportunity to select more than one race as their own. Ten years later, in the next census, there was an increase of 134 percent of people who checked boxes for both black and white.[9] Not only do we no longer see our *world* in simple color schemes, but we see *ourselves* this way too.

It's a welcome development for a church that has known Paul's observation that there is "neither Jew nor Greek . . . for you are all one in Christ Jesus" (Gal. 3:28). Yet it can also be a challenge. A generation ago, at the height of the church growth movement, the Homogeneous Unit Principle (HUP) ruled supreme (against a backdrop of criticism). Leaders were advised to design churches for people who looked, dressed, and thought alike. Why force people to cross racial or class boundaries? People, they reasoned, wanted to worship with their own kind. Once we lured them into the kingdom, then we could deal with the finer points of theology during the discipleship process.

It didn't always work out so simply, of course. Yet even now, the basic, perhaps cynical principles of marketing call out to those who would start new churches. Church planter David Swanson wrote:

> The HUP is seen less favorably these days, but it remains common for church planters to target culturally similar people. Categories such as *cultural elites, the creative class,* or *young professionals* may sound exotic but are often used to describe people most like the church planter.[10]

What's different is the changing hues of those who come through the doors, even if we're expecting cultural elites. The neighborhoods are changing. Pastors look across the rows of faces during their sermons and painfully realize they've prepared their teaching with the old, reliable stereotypes in mind—white suburban family with husband, wife, three kids, a dog, and two cars. The pastor wonders, *Is my focus too narrow? How do I preach to every kind of listener?*

Leaders are finding they must begin to think multiethnically, but that presents new challenges. Communicating with blocks of those who look and think as we do is one thing; communicating with a cross-section of the cultural landscape is another.

Paul, again thinking of Jews and Greeks, wrote:

> And he came and preached peace to you who were far off and peace to those who were near. For through him we both have access in one Spirit to the Father. So then you are no longer strangers and aliens, but you are fellow citizens with the saints and members of the household of God. (Eph. 2:17–19)

At some point church builders must look to the essence of our faith itself, rather than the most current marketing principles, to understand that the glue that holds us together is not found in cultural particulars but in Christ himself, who builds bridges rather than bolstering walls and who declares there are no longer any strangers or aliens—not in his eyes and therefore not in ours.

THE ADVENT OF POSTMODERNISM

The more postmodernism has been defined, the more confusion has abounded on the subject. It's an elusive concept with any number of definitions (which is itself true to the idea of postmodernism). While it originally emerged from the fields of art and architecture as a series of reactions against modernism in those fields, its impact is felt in virtually every other area of thinking in the current world.

APPROXIMATE YEARS	ERA	CHARACTERISTICS
30–100	Primitive Christianity	Apostolic teaching
100–600	Common Era	Classical Christianity formalized in creed councils and biblical canon establishment
600–1500	Medieval Era	Formation of Roman Christianity
1500–1750	Reformation	Birth and growth of Protestantism
1750–1980	Modern Era	Growth of denominations and mainline, liberal Protestantism; Vatican II; American Evangelicalism
1980–Present	Postmodern Era	Emergent, seeker sensitive, other movements

Source: Adapted from Robert Webber, *Ancient-Future Faith: Rethinking Evangelicalism for a Postmodern World* (Grand Rapids: Baker, 1999), 13.

Some see the defining moment for postmodernism as 1989, when the Berlin Wall came down. The symbolism was apt. In its rubble lay the neat divisions between democracy and communism, faith and reason, truth and exploration. Marxist communism was one more modern idea that was supposed to bring people to the promised land but led nowhere.

Postmodernism doesn't like walls of any kind. It questions compartmentalized thinking in favor of ambiguity. Spirituality is a topic, but it's never centered on a person such as Jesus or Muhammad. A survey by George Gallup and Timothy Jones at the turn of the millennium found people defining their spirituality with phrases such as the following:

"Calmness in my life"
"Something you really put your heart into"
"Believing in myself to make the right decisions"
"Having tension evolve into a whole spirit"
"The essence of my personal being since each person has his or her own essence"
"Your relationship to people and living positively"
"Living the life you feel is pleasing"
"The state of mind that some people have"
"Sensuality and one's senses; living by common sense"[11]

Postmodernity rejects the idea of objective and ultimate knowledge. Like Pilate it stands before the proclaimer of truth and scornfully asks, "What is truth?" Beginning, then, with the foundational thought that truth is unknowable and that all the big questions ultimately remain open, the discussion changes.

In a modernistic mind-set—from the age of reason to the Industrial Revolution to the mid- to late twentieth century—people assumed that each of life's greater questions had a logical, reachable answer. If it hadn't been found, we'd get to it sooner or later. Science bred confidence as it quickly cured illnesses, explained the mysteries of nature, and made life more comfortable. Even the horrors of the First World War were looked upon as the war that ended all wars. Humanity would outgrow petty bickering.

But that hope was crushed by the reality that science doesn't eliminate war; it only gives soldiers new weapons. The world after World War I was notable for a new worldly cynicism.

Later, as the world became more globally connected, ideas—including religious ones—began to interact and intersect. A single view of truth or God was easier when it lacked challenges in a human experience immersed only in one's own culture. But when worlds collided, it was more difficult to know who had the right ideas. The easiest answer to the question became *nobody*. When diversity rules, civility is served by treating all ideas as equals. And if no idea rises to the top, all sink to the bottom.

Postmodernism, at any rate, carries a preference for mystery, doubt, and flexibility. It's not the answers that count but the questions and the experience of the discussion. Nobody is right and nobody is wrong. If there is indeed an ultimate truth in postmodernism, it is community itself. We can't know the truth in the abstract, but we can know one another, and that becomes a goal in itself.

Fluidity is another central concept—life is a process, a road without destination and a journey worthwhile for its own sake. What I think today may not be what I think tomorrow, and that's fine because I'm content to live behind a veil of uncertainty.

It would be wrong to think of Christianity as more comfortable in either milieu—modernism or postmodernism. The ascent of science posed a challenge for faith for at least two centuries. Modernism had its own optimism, its own cherished future, and its own set of values, and it was a competing force for Christianity. High tide for the modernist challenge to faith was the 1925 Scopes Trial (the infamous Monkey Trial), when scientific and modern assumptions were used to ridicule fundamentalist biblical beliefs right out of the courtroom. Those with literal interpretations of Genesis discovered they no longer controlled the discussion. For the first time they were exposed to mockery and jeering. Christendom had reached the first moment of twilight.

If modernism scorned the idea of spiritual faith, postmodern thought actually reversed that direction. Modernism found that many of life's questions couldn't be found in a laboratory. Life is full of mystery and wonder. Spirituality itself, with all its mystery and ambiguity, was welcome and indeed sought, but that didn't mean Christianity, which of course attempts to resolve some of the mystery and clear up the ambiguities through its truth claims.

The churches can appeal to the postmodern mind through the beauty of the spiritual world they depict, but they must first overcome the inevitable objections: churches are an Old World anachronism; churches are too pedantic and rule oriented.

Warning: there isn't a program or curriculum that will help you become the apologist who can win over the postmodernist. It is in the DNA of this current philosophy to be elusive and subjective. How, then, do we engage the present-day philosopher? We do it by understanding the key issues of engagement while being able to weave our faith organically into conversations with truth and grace. Our goal isn't to win the momentary argument but to build bridges of dialogue that (we pray) will lead to conviction and ultimate transformation.

Toward those understandings, we must meet the postmodern mind at one bedrock, powerful point of challenge.

THE CHALLENGE TO TRUTH CLAIMS

Epistemology is the formal name for the study of the source of knowledge or truth. It represents the key parting of the ways between the Christian and postmodern viewpoints. It's very difficult to get around this difference, though some have tried. It's a foundational distinction.

Christianity makes claims that ultimate truth is not only knowable but known. This truth is found in the revelation of God to humanity as shown in the Scriptures. While certain mysteries remain—the nature of heaven, for example—the most burning questions have been answered through God becoming flesh in Jesus Christ. The Bible addresses and explains the human condition of sinful rebellion and offers the universal solution. It tells people who they are eternally and how they should live on earth.

Postmodernism calls these arrogant claims. It challenges the notion that truth can be found in any one source. What about other truth claims? Postmodern thinkers wouldn't necessarily claim there is *no* universal truth; they would merely insist it can only be found in glimmers, brief glimpses, relative to the context of our particular culture. Therefore Christians have a viable angle, but Hindus and Buddhists would as well, and all of these would be valid fragments of ultimate truth, whatever that may be.

Therefore we'll find an audience interested in truth and in spirituality. The problem comes either in its accepting *all* truth as valid or *none* of it. For if all religions are correct, then none of them are particularly correct. If Christianity claims one earthly life and Eastern religions claim many, then perhaps they cancel each other out. Perhaps they're both wrong. Christianity doesn't work as an alternative among many. It insists upon its unique status as God's revelation. The bedrock of Judaism, at the deepest foundation of the faith, is the first commandment that only one God be acknowledged and worshiped. This is our story; this is our irreducible minimum.

Postmodernists enjoy stories. This is one reason the Bible has appeal to them—it teaches through narrative, whether from the perspective of the nation of Israel or in the life and parables of Jesus. Postmodernists find in stories something tangible and personal, something suggestive of truth and yet still flexible and fluid. It is in this common ground that discussions can form and the Spirit and the Word can begin to do their mystical work.

An internal hunger for God resides in all of us, including postmodernists. We know that hunger can only be satisfied by a personal God. The spirituality of postmodernism welcomes some form of god much in the manner of the pantheon of gods in Acts 17. Kabbalistic Rabbi Rami Shapiro wrote: "People are starved for an experience of the divine. We go to church, or we go to synagogue, or we go to mosque or to temple or wherever we happen to go, and we hear talk about God. But we don't experience God. I think that's where mysticism comes in."[12]

As the church, it is our mission to express, demonstrate, and facilitate an understanding that Christ is the ultimate and full mediator between God and man. According to Robert Webber, the Christianity of postmodernity that "will speak effectively to a postmodern world is the one that emphasizes primary truths and authentic embodiment. The new generation is more interested in broad strokes than in detail, more attracted to an inclusive view of the faith than an exclusive view, more concerned with unity than diversity, more open to dynamic, growing faith than static fixed system, and more visual than verbal with a high level of tolerance and ambiguity."[13]

Postmodernists won't be won over by our airtight reasoning in structured theological debates. They will only be convinced by our embodiment of the life of Christ, spoken with truth and grace.

That's a challenge for us because we prize the reason behind our faith. Our epistemology is rooted in objective truth, but it is validated through experience. If your faith doesn't have a positive, experiential expression, making life more full and complete, you have little to show postmodernists that might make a difference in their view of the Christian faith.

On the other hand the truth is on our side. As Mark Yaconelli worded it:

This generation is longing for relationship, mystery, experience, passion, wonder, creativity, and spontaneity. In other words, they want to go past where the 'sidewalk ends.' They long for the place just beyond words, the shore of mystery. In other words, they're looking for Jesus.[14]

Let's help them complete that search.

───── FIVE ─────

UNDEFINED

The Changing Face of the Church's Focus

ELIZABETH GILBERT HAD NO IDEA HOW TO PICK UP THE PIECES.

She stood in her bathroom at 3 a.m. and wept. Not too long ago, she'd thought she had it all—a nice home, a husband she loved, and the prospect of starting a family. But now she wanted out of the marriage. What did this mean for her goals in life? Where should she turn?

She identified herself a Christian in a vague way, though she ruled out the conception of Jesus being the only path to salvation. Now, when she needed some kind of inner meaning, she fell to her knees and began to call out to God—whatever God might want to answer.

In time a voice seemed to answer her plea. The voice was her own, but a new calm and wise version. She described it as the Elizabeth Gilbert that would exist if she'd received nothing but love and certainty throughout her life. And this voice launched her on a quest that would be recounted in the book *Eat, Pray, Love*.[1] It spent a phenomenal six months on the *New York Times* best-seller list and eventually became a movie with Julia Roberts playing Gilbert.

The book offered a very attractive view of the life of faith, if not at all unique. The inner voice of herself taught her that God is simply a version of each of us, living inside us. The duty of life, she wrote, is to honor that personal slice of divinity.

Such a view, taking the most convenient versions of Christian prayer and adding healthy slices of Eastern religion and modern self-help mantras, is bound to appeal to people. It's a kind of cut-rate, no-frills spirituality that tells us everything we'd love to hear about ourselves without making many demands other than to honor some vague inner deity and maybe be kind to others.

But as Ross Douthat detailed in his book *Bad Religion*,[2] this is all part of the trend of "spiritual but not religious" seen in the postmodern landscape. Along with Gilbert we have Eckhart Tolle, Deepak Chopra, James Redfield, and even Oprah Winfrey urging people to reject traditional faith in favor of some form of inner awareness and peace. God is everywhere, particularly within. But he's not the most important issue; feelings are. Life is about ready happiness, self is paramount, and sin is an outmoded concept.[3]

The preacher's first response to all this, of course, is to prepare a sermon on false prophecy and the importance of sound doctrine. But it's crucial to see this moment in a wider perspective. Sound doctrine is, has been, and will always be essential. But if doctrine is somewhere in the discussion, we may be getting somewhere. Postmodernism welcomes conversations about spirituality. There is a bias against the ancient traditions of Christian belief, but just the same, there is an admission that we are spiritual creatures, that this world isn't enough, and that we need to be in search of greater meaning.

The father or stepfather of postmodernism—modernism itself —extended its bias to spirituality itself. It perhaps wouldn't have been admitted at the time, but there simply wasn't a great interest in the nature of the soul. Maybe the soul itself, people said, was an outgrown notion. The human creature was being mapped out, like the globe itself, and nothing answering to the description of soul was found—just flesh, bone, and a vast array of synapses that made up a brain.

With the forward march of science, there was a certain optimism about humanity and its future. Religion was seen as a past product of fear, natural to a creature who could not understand or control his environment. Now, with modern tools, we would harness the powers of nature, the unlimited abilities of the mind, and create utopia without the help of religious superstition.

As we've seen that didn't work out so well. As the twentieth century moved on, there was a realization that humanity may actually use the powers of nature (such as the atom) to destroy itself. Science and learning failed to answer the most basic questions. And the age-old belief systems kept rolling along like an ancient river.

Postmodernism ushered in a new era of spiritual interest. Some see the half-empty cup of pagan teachings advancing not only on the world but into the church itself. Others see a cup half-full because people are asking the right questions again. They're ready to talk. And our faith has always offered answers that satisfy hearts and souls. The church must see the present as an exciting invitation to dialogue.

THE TRIFECTA

While the above was transpiring, how did the church respond? In previous chapters we've described its response in terms of liminality (the disorientation of finding oneself caught between two stages of identity) and discontinuous change (nonorderly, disruptive transition). More specifically we might point to three identifiable periods of response within the church. We can break them down into the following chart.

	80s–90s	LATE 90s–2000	2000–2010	DESIRED CULMINATION
Trend	Attractional	Missional	Gospel	**Incarnational**
Emphasis	Orthopathy	Orthopraxy	Orthodoxy	**Holistic Gospel**

THE ATTRACTIONAL MOVEMENT

During the 1980s the church world was buzzing about user-friendly and seeker-sensitive churches. As Baby Boomers settled into adult and family life, it was clear that the church could no longer simply open its doors and draw a crowd. The old hymns and detailed, doctrinal sermons suddenly seemed dusty and ineffective. Leaders such as Rick Warren and Bill Hybels built new models of churches, designed to appeal to the people the church was losing.

A young Hybels had canvased neighborhoods and discovered that nonattenders didn't want to dress up. They disliked the idea of a collection plate, and they didn't enjoy old-time music. They wanted sermons that spoke to the practical problems of modern life. Predictably the churches that resulted immediately attracted accusations of selling out the cross, preaching cheap grace, and the rest. But the sermons of Warren and Hybels were actually orthodox and balanced in their theology. It was probably the radical new feel of the worship service—more like a rock concert than grandpa's old church service—that invited complaints from those uncomfortable with the changes.

Attractional Churches were pragmatic in realizing that something with higher energy and more creativity was necessary to entice visits on Sunday mornings. Indeed many churches added services that weren't on Sunday *or* in the morning. The message to the watching world was, "Come give us another try. Wear your jeans. Keep your wallet in your pocket. You might even find yourself moving to the groove of the band—and staying awake during the serious content, now presented in skits and with colorful, PowerPoint-delivered talks." The emphasis was on creating a safe place to explore the Christian faith. The hope was that many would reimagine a faith more personal and relevant than stuck in a particular denominational flavor.

Lyle Schaller considered it all nothing less than a new Reformation. His list of distinctives included the following:

> Contemporary, creative worship; new resources from a wide range of agencies; market-driven planning; lay-empowered ministry; the emergence of approximately four thousand Protestant megachurches; an emphasis on prayer and spiritual formation; staff teams replacing the superstar preacher; the flattening of hierarchical ecclesiastical structures; the rapid increase in independent churches, numbering twenty thousand churches with 15 million adherents; and lay-led Bible study groups.[4]

The real contribution of the attractional era was the shift in perspective—starting to see the church from an outsider's point of view. And there were many success stories, not only from Hybels's Willow Creek Community Church and Warren's Saddleback Church, but from a dense flowering of newly planted churches across America, as well as established congregations adding so-called seeker services. If the new forms inevitably moved from fresh and creative to highly predictable, this was an era that finally overthrew the sameness of the old structures and got the church thinking about the people it was clearly failing to reach. The motive for such radical transformation was a renewed passion (*orthopathos*) for the unchurched.

Still, the ecstatic announcements of a new Reformation were premature. The church had not arrived or solved all its problems. If it was going to survive past the last vestiges of Christendom, it would need to keep working, keep growing, keep thinking outside the box.

MISSIONAL MOVEMENT

The next generation took the changes of the attractional movement for granted. Sure, there was new music, a more casual approach, maybe more comfortable seating. But wasn't something missing? The Boomer parents were less likely to see it. They knew there had already been terrific changes to bring the church up to date.

But their children—the so-called Baby Busters—understood that the New Testament they were reading was about much more than great worship, more even than effective evangelism that could reach the unchurched. *Mission* was the missing ingredient.

Weren't we bringing in new believers for a purpose, namely, to send them out? Pastors spoke of huge numbers of worshipers who came every week, enjoyed the services, and went home again. Getting them that far had been a victory worth celebrating. But there had to be more than this to what we were about. The next wave was inevitable, and its focus was inevitable: action in the world, service, significant ministry. Come and hear must, at some point, become go and do.

One issue of the attractional era was the targeted demographic. Seekers were often understood as living in the suburbs, as being middle- to upper-middle class, and as being a lot like the Christian leaders attempting to reach them. There were exceptions, but many of the new campuses were built with suburban America surrounding them on all sides. This, too, created a certain level of backlash.

If the Attractional Church was about being loud and proud through flashy worship services, the missional movement was distinctive in its new humility. Proximity to genuine human need, of course, will have that effect. It's a result of the *orthopraxy* of being in someone's life—not simply performing or pitching a better Christian faith, but actually living it out side by side.

Also, with the perceived dangers of breeding spectator Christians in large megachurch auditoriums—applauding, perhaps lifting their hands, and then going home until the next service—the time was right for a renewal of the idea of Christian discipleship lived out in the mission of God (*missio dei*, the phrase that seems to be the forerunner of the buzz word *missional*).

The word took on a life of its own so rapidly that there's a great deal of confusion with regard to its meaning. Because most churches have missions programs, it can easily be confused with the established idea of sending out missionaries or of simply enlarging the missions program. Others worry that they detect the scent of liberalism, specifically the nineteenth-century social gospel resurrected again to reduce Christianity to social work. At some point, someone quotes Francis of Assisi: "At all times preach the gospel. If necessary, use words." One problem is there's no evidence he ever said this.[5] Another is that such an idea sounds like mere social action for those embarrassed to admit they follow Jesus.

Missional doesn't mean any of those things. It's more focused on living out the work of Jesus in this world. That implies spending time among the hurting rather than donating to causes for them. It means placing a focus on healing and helping in the places where it's most needed. And it takes the focus away from building a better mousetrap with the flashiest worship service and on to putting the church into action making a difference. The Attractional Church would have programs for doing this and perhaps healthy involvement in these programs. Groups would regularly serve at food banks or go on overseas trips to build orphanages in Haiti—all good works.

Missional Churches, on the other hand, organized themselves around such things and tried to get everyone involved rather than a few with special compassion. Lesslie Newbigin has helped the church understand that mission is what the church is *about* rather than an activity it pursues. In a post-Christendom world, he discovered, nothing can be taken for granted. The church must *be* a mission rather than having missions. It must embody its message.[6]

Dr. Charles Swindoll has told a story of Puritan times in England, when Oliver Cromwell was in power. Times were tough, and there was a shortage of silver for coins. Cromwell sent his men into the churches to round up a little excess silver. "None there but in the statues," said the silver searchers. "There are statues of the saints guarding each corner of the church."

"Fine," Cromwell said. "Melt 'em down. We need to put those saints into circulation."

The story captures the transition from Attractional to Missional Churches. The saints are out of their churchly corners and into circulation in the world, where the needs are practical. But do we have to choose one way or the other? I don't think so. Your church can be the best model of an Attractional Church yet have the heart of a Missional Church. We always turn to Jesus for guidance—Jesus who drew the crowds with spectacular miracles, and then taught, healed, and fed them while they were assembled. But he always went to where the people were. He was missional.

GOSPEL RESURGENCE

Within two decades the church rediscovered a powerful renaissance in worship style and a renewal of community mission. Had the church found its happily ever after? Of course not—it always continues to grow, find new forms, and reequip itself to each new generation. But in the resurgence of gospel emphasis, Millennials have advanced the revolution by returning to historical *orthodoxy*.

Why would gospel resurgence follow from the previous movements? Perhaps as a healthy refocus on the truth on which all of this is grounded. The main attraction is Jesus. The mission is Jesus. The gospel is the good news that we proclaim in everything we do.

This resurgence of our basic theme, beginning around the turn of the millennium, has (as in the time preceding it) taken a common church word and rebaptized it as a buzz word, using it in so many contexts that it's not always clear what people mean when they speak of a new Gospel Church. Recently the word has almost become a requirement for Christian book titles.

In basic terms, however, this is a time of getting our doctrine right. For one thing, the rising secular influence within church leadership brought doctrinal issues into question. Also controversies began to arise as newer, more radical church leaders, such as Brian McLaren, challenged the old, acceptable boundaries, calling for "new doctrines for a new century."[7]

Again the assumptions of a postmodern perspective have brought the church to a time of reemphasizing the orthodox basics of the gospel—thus a gospel resurgence. This hasn't been a distinct new direction for the church in the sense of the preceding two movements, but it's more a moment to stop and taken inventory of our heritage and essentials, affirming that we are the same eternal church regardless of our processes as they are renewed and reshaped.

Gospel was the one word that could take in all the facets of our reason for existence. It became noun, verb, adjective, adverb, subject, and predicate. I recently heard a pastor refer to "gospeling our relationships." The word was as historically orthodox and safe as *missional* had been vaguely liberal and unsettling. Yet George Barna tells us that only 31 percent of respondents had an accurate understanding of what the word *gospel* meant.[8] It's all too easy to strip a word of any powerful meaning by overusing or misusing it.

Orthodoxy movements throughout Christian history have followed hard on new-emphasis movements. The attractional movement was a time of *orthopathos*, or right passion (right feeling). Attendance had been declining, and if we wanted people to attend church, it had to feel right. There needed to be some emotion. The missional movement was about *orthopraxis*, or right practice (right action). And the gospel-centered movement is about the most familiar *ortho* of all: *orthodoxy* (right belief).

At different times, then, we've focused on three areas of personhood: the heart (attractional), the hands (missional), and the head (gospel). Putting it that way we can easily understand that all of these are good but partial attempts to fulfill our destiny as God's people.

The Bible gives us one sentence to cover the maturation process of the Savior: "Jesus increased in wisdom and in stature and in favor with God and man" (Luke 2:52). The full gospel must be given to the full individual—heart, soul, mind, and body. We need to think more holistically. So where do we go from here?

INCARNATIONAL CHRISTIANITY

I submit that our future is to be found in incarnational living. We find ourselves in the midst of the conflict where a hurting world lies. We have formed safe, authentic communities where the unaffiliated may come to process out loud their life and faith, no matter how messy it may be. We have shown a willingness to involve ourselves in the lives of others. We have reaffirmed the gospel metanarrative that has always defined who we are: "The faith that was once for all delivered to the saints" (Jude 3).

What we need now is to find what it means to live in the world as true friends of sinners. Jesus drew sharp criticism for attending dinners and parties with sinners and tax collectors. True incarnational living is committed to dwelling in the midst of those who need the light.

In chapter 3 we discussed Philippians 2:7 as the basis for incarnational life and ministry. It's worth revisiting it in our present context. Paul tells us that Christ "emptied himself" into flesh to become one of us and thus accomplish what could only be done in person.

Though he was God he knew what it meant to grow up in a community of no repute (Nazareth, from which it was said, in John 1:46, that nothing good could possibly come). It was no less than God in the ghetto. "Being born in the likeness of men" (Phil. 2:7) speaks to the *orthopraxy* of Jesus. He chose to cast away his elite heavenly status to identify, not only with humanity, but with the *least* of humanity.

As Jesus took on the cultural flavor of his surroundings, so the Attractional Church identifies with its target culture. In some sense we must be them to reach them. He "humbled himself" (Phil. 2:8), creating in his life the attraction of humility by removing any walls that would separate him from fallen humanity. Jesus was the embodiment of seeker sensitive.

Finally Jesus is the gospel in every sense of the word. He is the good news; he is the orthodoxy. He is our doctrine, our foundation, our basis for everything. "Even death on a cross" (v. 8) speaks of his sacrificial death as the culmination of his reaching into this world and of what the gospel finally demands. Jesus, then, is attractional, missional, gospel, and, above all and through all and in all, incarnational. In every era of the Resurgent Church, we seem to capture some aspect of who he was and what he intends for us, but we never seem to see the full spectrum of the God-man who takes on our essence to identify with us, who comes seeking us with love and compassion, and who offers us all the meaning of gospel truth and hope. I believe the church, in these demanding times, must do better. We must capture, as closely as possible, the full essence of his incarnational life and service in this world.

It's easier said than done; that's why it's so infrequently been done over the last twenty centuries. The built-in enigma is that committed believers with this mission are those who are being transformed into the image of Christ daily. As time goes by they are more and more different from the sinners they're called to befriend. That would present a problem with any ordinary reckoning of friendship. But we trust the work of the Holy Spirit to empower us beyond our own abilities to minister. We count on his limitless compassion to give us a love we could never attain on our own. And when, against all odds, incarnational friendships occur, God is glorified and the world takes notice.

An incarnational presence in the world calls for a contextualized and personalized gospel. Again the church must always affirm its doctrinal essentials, but it must decide what does the gospel do in this declining, crime-ridden neighborhood? What does it mean to be Jesus in this area of town or that one? Missional is about going, but incarnational is about staying and getting the job done. Missional is God loving and speaking to a lost world. Incarnational is about God sending his Son and being willing to make the fullest commitment, to the point of the cross.

Therefore we follow in the example of Jesus, whose earthly life was the model of this concept. Like him we bring full compassion and a willingness to heal. But that's always balanced by the ministry of teaching, of being a voice in context, pointing the way to salvation. Preaching and healing, grace and truth, words and deeds: all of these must be kept in balance.

I've put together the following statement describing how we can carry out our mission as the church, building on the context of the movements that have brought us here: *Our task is to passionately and intentionally live among unbelievers and/or the unaffiliated with grace and truth.*

- Passionately and intentionally (*orthopathy*): We bring the right emotion: being so in love with God's lost and wandering children that we will remove every man-made barrier and take every possible step to create an environment where these children will want to explore his truth and be reconciled to him.

- Live among unbelievers and/or the unaffiliated (*orthopraxy*): We pursue the right practice, extending daily life to choosing friends and using time in ways that serve the kingdom. The goal is to see our lives on mission 24/7. The key phrase here is *live among.* Join a yoga class, coach a Little League baseball team, find your favorite coffee shop, or learn to live with and among them. Mission is no longer an excursion but a life of immediacy. Mission becomes what we do and who we are to such an extent that we no longer even use the words *going on mission* because we *live on mission.* We simply speak of life, which is defined as serving Christ at every point of need.
- With grace and truth (*orthodoxy*): These are more than decorative words. They refer to a careful balance between preaching and healing. Throughout Christian history these two have been set against each other as if they presented an either/or choice. Which did Jesus prefer? The answer is "yes." He affirmed both fully and entirely walking the walk and talking the talk. The moment prioritized the task. In studying the early church, we find the same balance between preaching and service. Right practice should never call for wrong doctrine, but instead affirm it. And right doctrine always calls for right action.

The late British Anglican scholar John R. W. Stott brought all of this together rather well in one statement:

[Jesus] sends us into the world, as the Father sent him into the world. . . . In other words our mission is to be modeled on his. Indeed all authentic mission is incarnational mission. It

demands identification without loss of identity. It means entering other people's worlds as he entered ours, though without
compromising our Christian convictions, values, or standards.[9]

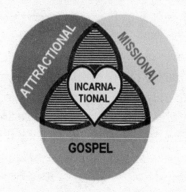

It will be uncomfortable because it has been undefined. This
mission presupposes a tension we must learn to manage: how to
do more than one thing at a time and to do them with excellence.
We must discover how to be missional, biblical, and practical in
the community to which God has called us in order to create the
new kingdom community he insists upon seeing for our future.
The tension will create friction. There will be disagreements and
diverging paths and sometimes failure on our part. But it's a long
game, a marathon, not a sprint. The more we raise up churches to
live incarnationally in their corners of the world, the more Christ
will shine through. And when that happens, history changes.

PART TWO

RESURGENT

IT HAS TO HAPPEN AND, IN FACT, IS HAPPENING. CHURCHES ARE PICK-ing up on the currents of a new world, they're understanding what they see, and they're reequipping themselves. They're not simply trying to ride it out until somehow the comfortable past returns and reassures them. They begin with the assumption that there's no way to outwait the future.

These churches are hard at work. They're refitting, reworking, and reimagining what the body of Christ is supposed to be, not just for today, but forever and from the very beginning.

These churches have a way of peering over the horizon and into the future while doubling down on the truths they've found in the book of Acts. They're innovative yet doctrinally scrupulous.

These churches have dared to question the way they've always done things and discovered there are, in fact, better ways for those willing to pay the price of change.

These churches have looked upon the greatest cultural challenges yet faced by Christianity and caught sight of the greatest opportunities. They know that throughout the history of our faith, times of challenge have led to the times of our greatest breakthroughs.

These churches have shared some specific, thoroughly intriguing solutions, and you'll find them in this section. There are no easy formulas here. No seven steps to happily ever after. What you'll find instead are key challenging paradigm changes that demand our openness and force us to question many of the ideas we've held dear for so long.

Yet these churches are making it work. We call them *resurgent*. How do we define a resurgent church? I believe there are at least four distinctives:

1. A resurgent church is modeled after its maker: Jesus. He is the God in flesh, and we are called to be Jesus in flesh to the world.
2. A resurgent church is shaped by its culture. Understanding our context gives form to our expression.
3. A resurgent church mobilizes its people. It measures success not by how many it gathers in but how many it sends out.
4. A resurgent church, because of the above, is organized around reaching its community and the nations.

I have studied churches that look like this. How many more will rise up to join them?

FROM SET TO CONTEXT

No Size Fits All

*They heard the loud noise, everyone came running,
and they were bewildered to hear their own
languages being spoken by the believers.*
ACTS 2:6 NLT

I GREW UP IN A TIGHT SQUARE BOX.

The funny thing is I had no idea that was the case. If you spend all of your time in a shoebox, it never occurs to you there are other places. The cardboard walls define life's boundaries. If you're a fish who spends his whole life in an aquarium, the universe measures about twelve inches by six inches. And you imagine you've got things figured out.

Actually my box world was just church. It was a carefully defined enclosure that, for my context, made perfect sense.

I knew this because I visited other churches occasionally, and I was immediately comfortable. Those boxes were just like my box. They had long rows of seats. They had certain musical instruments. They had choirs who wore certain apparel. And there was preaching that sounded very similar wherever I went. I knew their songs and lingo.

Those were the superficial similarities. But it went deeper. I had no idea how boxy my idea of the church was.

Then we moved to Zambia.*

We learned to think outside the box very quickly when it came to what a church was, how it looked, and how it functioned.

Our intention was to live in south central Africa for the rest of our lives. We planned to raise our family and build our church life there. But there we were, our bags unpacked, and it felt as if everything we knew was wrong. It felt as if we'd ordered an elephant and received an ostrich. Sure, we knew the culture would be different. We knew the people would come from very different life experiences. But church was church. Wasn't it?

Here's what I think. If you're planning to serve in vocational ministry in any capacity—even in the box of your own hometown—you should be required to spend your first two years serving internationally in an entirely different culture. It's a whack on the side of the head that will jumble all your neatly arranged thoughts and cause you to reassemble them.

I'm proud of my theological training. It was excellent in so many ways, but it definitely prepared me to be a pastor in a little church on Main Street, Christendom, USA. I knew exactly how to be a mostly successful pastor in a certain well-trodden culture. But I had no idea where to start when the lid came off the box. We weren't in Kansas anymore, as Dorothy told Toto, and we didn't even have a yellow-brick road to follow.

Of course I hadn't been trained specifically as a *missionary*. That was the difference. If I had, I would have spent time working

---

* My wife, Lori, is my soul mate and colleague in ministry. Together we moved our two kids, ages three and five, to this mission field. And there a third child was born. We call him our African American child, though his skin is white.

through a host of ideas such as contextualization, enculturation, worldviews, and syncretism.

We routinely teach our missionaries these things out of necessity, and they avoid the culture shock I experienced. They go into every kind of social setting, into every people group, and share the gospel with remarkable success. Why shouldn't we train our stateside leaders the same way? Eddie Gibbs commented that, within Christendom, church life and church mission became separated to their mutual impoverishment. Our urgent task, he said, is to reconnect them and demonstrate a "missional ecclesiology."[1] If there is one Lord, one faith, and one baptism, shouldn't we be one church? Shouldn't there be a powerful consistency between church life and church mission?

When we read Acts 2:6 we're struck by the power and emotion of the passage: "Loud noise . . . came running . . . bewildered." This was more than a quiet teaching of theological concepts. It was a life-changing message taking root in the hearts and minds of those who couldn't get there fast enough to satisfy their curiosity.

In the West we've been so mind-and-reason oriented that we've sometimes forgotten that people need to *hear and feel* the gospel in their own language. This is the beauty of what God did at Pentecost—that is, he spoke in all languages rather than one. To hear in our own language means to hear from the very heart and worldview of a specific individual.

We need to see as God sees so we can speak as he spoke at Pentecost, to do the hard work of digging into the soul of our culture, understanding its yearnings, and overcoming the many barriers we've created so we can express our message holistically, rationally, emotionally, and physically in such a way that people come running again.

It won't happen because of a set model dictated by denominations or trends or convenience. It will happen through *contextualized* models perfectly mated to the worldviews we find. In other words, our journey is from set to context, from presuppositions to compassionate listening and response.

Timothy Keller defined *contextualization* as "giving people the Bible's answers, which they may not all want to hear, to questions about life that people in their particular time and place are asking, in language and forms they can comprehend, and through appeals and arguments with force they can feel, even if they reject them."[2] Contextualization is the gospel and its advocate entering into a culture, identifying with them in all ways possible, and serving as agents of transformation in the lives of people.

And that's a problem. Because we really like our simple, just-add-water recipes. We don't mind using exactly the same model that a famous hyped megachurch has used, because it's the quick results we're after. If it's working over there, surely it will pack them in over here. Within our own tight square box we must admit that approach has sometimes worked in the past. But we can also guess that at all times, in all places, the spirit of God would rather lead us creatively and uniquely to build in the context of our community wherever and whenever it may be. The God who knows the hairs on every head doesn't deal in templates and ready-made packages. He knows hearts, he knows communities, and he never reaches out to anyone in exactly the same way.

We have to learn to listen and to understand. Church growth fads and formulas will no longer work if we wish to penetrate the cultures of our day.

INSIDE THE OVERLAP

This diagram is a simple illustration of what has been happening as well as what needs to happen. The community has one life (or more accurately, as we'll see, a large network of lives through subcultures); the church has a separate one. As Christendom has lost its authority, the church has felt increasingly alienated from its culture, more anxious and uncertain, and gradually distanced itself. Sometimes the kingdom of God is perceived as having a high wall and a moat.

For many churches this has not been just a cultural shift but a physical, geographical shift. Beginning in the mid-twentieth century, urban churches began to relocate to the suburbs for reasons ranging from crime to urban decay to simply following the exodus of their members. But here we're speaking mainly of the *cultural* differences between the church and its community.

In the next diagram we see that the Resurgent Church is moving back toward an overlap with the community it serves. This comes only through incarnational interactivity. We could say that the Attractional Church of recent decades attempted the reverse: draw in the community and then culturize the new converts.

Clearly there are limits to reaching a community that way. But as we engage in living and working among people, building relationships in context, the overlap in the diagram begins to develop. Within that overlap God does great work. It's the sweet spot of true incarnational mission, simply following the missionary model we would use anywhere else in the world. The Resurgent Church moves more within the world's circle, and if it shows itself loving and compassionate and compelling, the world responds.

What about compromise? Isn't it inevitable that when light has fellowship with darkness, to use the apostle John's words, we lose our hold on the essential doctrines? No, not at all. Incarnational Churches are proving that compromise need never be an issue. It's again important to affirm that we hold fast to our beliefs and historical identity as followers of Jesus Christ—and to affirm that following him will lead us to where the people are. We learn how they speak and think rather than expect them to come and learn about us. And we need not sell out the gospel any more than Jesus did.

Every church body needs to have a clear, articulated understanding of *who* it is and *where* it is. Where is that ministry place—the overlap? If there is none, the church needs to find ways to respond intelligently to its culture. Incarnational means going into the world to put on the flesh of the people we love and wish to reach. As we've seen in earlier chapters, Jesus entered the context, not only of humanity itself, but of a specific culture at a specific time and place. As he spoke of a new kingdom and a new, abundant life, he was sharing meals with people of all kinds, frequenting village squares, and making friends as he made a difference.

The *where*: Each church needs an ethnographic profile of its community (the where part of the equation). It should be prepared by those who have updated demographic studies and tabulations of the specific area around the church's footprint. What is the median age? Income? Racial profile? Where are jobs found? See the section near the end of this chapter, "Moving from Set to Context," for a better understanding of key zones to consider in a particular cultural context.

Sometimes we assume we know our little corner of the map simply because we live there. But invariably, as people get their hands on a community profile, they're likely surprised on many fronts by the information they find.

Understanding the community around us is the first step to contextualization, when the church adapts its message and its voice to address a particular mission without compromising the gospel essentials.

The *who*: Churches need to have a clear understanding of their own identity, not only in terms of their doctrine and goals (such as to glorify God and to build disciples), but also their own demographics. How many active members or attenders do we have? What is the median age? Income? Values? Passions? Gifts? What sets our church apart from other local churches?

It may take some work and some study, but leaders need to compile their own church ethnography.

SYNERGY

Let's look again at the circle diagram. We spoke of a sweet spot of ministry in the place where church and community—the who and the where—overlap. We can put a finer point on that. The overlap can be thought of as a church's *ethnographic synergy.*

We usually define synergy in business terms—a zone where two distinct businesses can intersect to mutual advantage. In ethnographic terms, we mean a place where the congregation is gifted, blessed, and passionate in such a way that these drives align with the community and its own needs and passions.

Again, this is as exciting as a cross-cultural international missions experience. We have to see ourselves as missionaries to post-Christendom. And there's nothing dull or routine about that. It's where the miracles happen—the front lines of kingdom work—where we see God clearly on the move. The church is doing what its people do best and with the greatest enthusiasm. The community sees the church as being relevant, useful, and attractive. Friendships blossom. Positive and creative things happen, and the overlap grows.

Charles Kraft, in his book *Christianity in Culture*,[3] offered a simple but brilliant example of how this is already being done: Bible translation. Formal-equivalence Bibles give literal, word-for-word translations from the Greek text. So, for example, we would read the admonitions of both Peter and Paul to "greet one another with a holy kiss" (Rom. 16:16).

A dynamic-equivalence translation, however, is more concerned about *key thoughts* than precise wording. That is, what did this verse mean to those who heard it, and how would we say that to our culture? J. B. Phillips paraphrased the above verse as "Give each other a hearty handshake all round."

The first approach is essential for Christians in their own study and spiritual growth. Serious Bible students want to know precisely what the apostles said, and they'll work through the idioms to find it. But the second method does a better job of speaking to people in the community at large. Nonbelievers might be a little wary of being met at the door with something called a holy kiss on their first visit!

Kraft suggested we need "dynamic equivalence churches."[4]

That means doing what Bible translators do: building bridges between ancient doctrines and modern communities. They need to find what the ancient faith meant to its founders and then present it in ways that make the best sense in a new environment.

Of course, there will never be universal agreement between essential scriptural truth and what is cultural, fluid, and flexible. It can only drive us to know our Scriptures and our beliefs all the more authoritatively so we can rightly handle the Word of truth (2 Tim. 2:15) in its application to modern community life. The best way to avoid compromise is to be clear on where the boundaries are.

To our shame Madison Avenue's army of advertisers could teach us our business here. They understand both circles—church and community—because they hope to sell their wares to everyone. They understand how to speak to any audience in words that resonate. When Hollywood releases a film, it prepares various trailers that speak to audience segments. One might be geared toward males, featuring the movie's action scenes; another might spotlight the emotional or romantic elements they perceive as appealing to a female audience. Before any movie is released, the studios have a precise idea about what market they're trying to reach, and they proceed intelligently.

This shouldn't spark another "marketing the church" debate. We never need to reduce the gospel to simplistic talking points for advertisement purposes. But we do need to bring to our efforts intentionality and an intelligent understanding of the people we're trying to communicate with. Like effective advertisers we need to know who these people are, what they care about, and what they dream about.

In one of the great Incarnational Church passages in the New Testament, Paul discussed how he made himself a "servant to all, that I might win more of them." He became as a Jew for the Jews' sake, and as a gentile for the gentiles' sake; he became weak to reach the weak, and so on. "I have become all things to all people, that by all means I might save some. I do it all for the sake of the gospel, that I may share with them in its blessings" (1 Cor. 9:22–23).

To read the life of Paul is to see that he did that very thing throughout his ministry. But how effective would he have been if he hadn't been a worldly, educated man who was fluent in the various cultures he encountered?

TRIBES AND SUBCULTURES

Tag Media and Ink, a marketing enterprise in the Phoenix, Arizona, metropolitan area, established the Joshua Survey, a demographic community study for church leaders trying to serve their neighborhoods. The metric discovers all the basic indicators and offers insights into the needs, preferences, and opportunities found in specific communities.

This group, part of a growing trend of community demographic study for churches, identifies seventy tribes and twenty-one life stages to put together an ethnographic profile of a community. It's the same kind of data marketing agencies use for predicting behavior and purchasing patterns. If we were to enter an unreached province in South America, one of the first questions we'd ask would be, "What are the tribes in this area? What are their beliefs and customs?" Then we'd want to know something about the life stages, rites of passage, and other descriptors of the people we were trying to reach.

We would survey the land or, more precisely, the people. Every church needs to revert to square one and pretend it knows nothing at all about its community. Then it needs to begin learning. Groups such as Tag Media and others (some of them denominational agencies) can provide skilled, effective assistance in providing the information we need about the tribes and life stages in the spiritual wilderness around us.

But the profile won't be simple and consistent. If we use the help of qualified sociologists and demographers, we'll discover that what we call community is, in fact, a collective of smaller communities—formally called subcultures and sometimes thought of as tribes. Your community may contain a biker subculture, for example. It has its own dress code, values, traditions, and vocabulary. Some western communities have a cowboy subculture, and churches are developing strategies to reach it.

Urban areas know all about geeks and goths. Alcoholics Anonymous, single parents, homeschool families—all of these can take on the distinguishing characteristics of subcultures. Of course in the increasing melting pot of our cities, we can't ignore ethnic and national subcultures in staggering varieties and numbers. It's possible to do what we've thought of as international missions within our own zip code. Is the church going to seize these opportunities? Is it really interested? Incarnational, Resurgent Churches are community-minded, but they also seek to have a global reach.

In our survey of people groups and subcultures, we might stumble over one of the largest tribes of all without realizing it: the church itself, a classic subculture. Its beliefs and values and traditions are extremely well defined. As we attempt to understand who the people are who fill in our landscape, we need to see ourselves as others see us and realize that we, too, can present the bewildering obstacles of language and mores, even when people come out of curiosity.

The incarnational mind-set draws us into the lives of others, and this helps to break down those walls.

No longer does my church life occur in a box. To be honest, there are moments when I miss the simplicity of my earliest church experiences—the predictability of it, the shared sense of subculture. But then I think of the adventure that was in no way possible within the limits of old-school church life. I hear the stories of our members as they have another experience sharing the gospel, and I'm more thankful than ever to grow up in a time when the false security of Christendom lulled us all to sleep.

Jesus wants to go to all the corners of the earth, and he wants to start just across town. He speaks across language barriers. He speaks across ethnicity and life experience gaps. He appeals to every culture humanity can form, so we can go forward with passion and enthusiasm. It's going to be exciting to see one Lord manifest in countless people groups. Numerous agencies, denominations, and parachurch establishments are available to help churches understand their context.

Zones of Identity

Here are a few groups and sources of information to help you begin to understand your community cultural context. Check also with your denomination, ministry organization, or agency.

Barna Group:** https://www.barna.org/dloads/barna-report-cities
-2015-detail

City Data: http://www.city-data.com

Joshua Survey: http://joshuasurvey.com

North American Mission Board (Southern Baptist):** http://www
.namb.net/namb1pb2col.aspx?pageid=8590000141

People Groups:*** www.peoplegroups.org

Percept Group: http://www.perceptgroup.com

Relocation Essentials: http://relocationessentials.com

US Census: http://www.census.gov/people/

Zip Skinny: http://www.makeuseof.com/tag/zipskinny/

MOVING FROM SET TO CONTEXT

Church leaders find themselves looking at a major paradigm shift as they consider going contextual. What are the major questions they face?

Peter Drucker, an influential leader among leaders, was credited with saying, "Once the facts are clear the decisions jump out at you." So it's a matter of doing the work, getting the facts.

The church needs to ask questions in five zones. In each, the questions are limitless, especially since each question immediately raises a host of subquestions. Don't get lost! I'm going to suggest a few starter questions. Once you understand each zone, you can customize your mission and your vision. You'll see a lot of *what* questions in the example below, but these only lead us to *why* questions. You must think deeply about your culture.

---

*Limited number of cities available.

** Information available only to Southern Baptist churches.

***Identifying unreached people groups that may live in your area could be a valuable link in your global strategies.

- **Faces of Diversity**: Get a snapshot of the worldview-shaping elements that have made the people who they are.
  - ~ What is the ethnic diversity of the community? What are the top three ethnic groups within your church's reach?
  - ~ What is the lifestyle of the community? (Rural, urban, suburban, etc.)
  - ~ What is the generational gap? Composites?
  - ~ What is the education level? Opportunities for continuing education?
- **Family Structure**: Understanding the family unit and relational structures will show a deeper dimension of your people. Stresses, interests, and passions will be revealed. According to the Joshua Survey, there are seventy possible household profiles and twenty-one life stages.
  - ~ What is the typical marital status of the community?
  - ~ What is the annual household income?
  - ~ What are the age demographics of the home?
  - ~ What is the life stage of the community?
- **Fun Times**: Discretionary time and money offer powerful windows of opportunity for developing relationships, which are best formed while people are decompressing from the more serious pursuits.
  - ~ What are the favorite vehicles for physical fitness? (Yoga, biking, hiking, gym, etc.)
  - ~ What are the people's dreams and aspirations revealed in neighborhood parties and happy-hour conversations at the bar?
  - ~ Where does your community spend its discretionary income? (Art, electronics, sports, entertainment, travel?)
  - ~ What topics seem to energize people during casual conversations?

- **Felt Needs:** In some way all people express their deeper needs and cravings. These felt needs are not the church's ultimate concern but simply an effective way to move toward eternal issues.
  - ~ What are the primary stressors in the community? (Speak with city government, local counselors, even the local news.)
  - ~ What are the projections for the local economy? How do those influence lifestyles?
  - ~ What is the political climate of the community?
  - ~ What is the socioeconomic status of the community?

Each of these four zones opens the way to the fifth, which is the church's ultimate business, namely, the state of community faith.

- **Faith Preference:** This is where we catch glimpses beyond the visible practiced faith into the true, honest conditions of people's souls.
  - ~ In times of crisis, what faith expressions are instinctively sought out?
  - ~ What is the historical faith of the community? What about the present day?
  - ~ How, where, and to whom do people give their charitable gifts?
  - ~ What style of worship seems to be the preference on key religious holidays?
  - ~ Begin with some of the questions above, add new ones that occur to you, and begin the process of writing an ethnographic profile of the people in your community. Don't get bogged down in details! Limit your profile to no more than three sentences.

ETHNOGRAPHIC PROFILES OF TWO COMMUNITIES WITH INCARNATIONAL CHURCHES		
NAME	Mosaic	Grace Point
LOCATION	Los Angeles, California	Bentonville, Arkansas
SURVEY DISTANCE	1-mile radius target area	7-mile radius target area
DESCRIPTIVE	Artistic dreamers	Corporate climbers
FACES	Strongly urbanicity (urban, dense); age range 24–35; mixed races with high diversity of all nationalities. Anglo, Hispanic, Asian are largest, with projected increase in Native American by 2020. 29% are college graduates.	Suburban; age range 36–55; large Anglo population with growing African American and Hispanic. Over 400 Asian descent households. 22% are college graduates.
FAMILY	49% Singles/no kids with nontraditional family structures. 37% married. At the turn of the millennium, more people in the entertainment industry attended Mosaic than any other church in Los Angeles.[5]	60% Married, school-age kids with traditional family structures. 25% never-married singles
FUN	Entertainment and arts; night life; many go to bed at 3:00 a.m.	Fitness, community sports. Lake and nature activities.
FELT NEEDS	Cash flow is tight; quality relationships; hopes and dreams realized or dashed. Single moms carry the highest stress levels with deeper levels of poverty than the national average.	Many of the trappings of wealth and success have pulled families in many directions, adding undue stress ("affluenza"). High stress and workloads make discretionary time scarce.
FAITH	Historically Christian with over 48% not involved. Well above the national average. Nontraditional churches are preferred when choosing.	High levels of notional to nominal Christians; the 400 Asian families and increased influx of non-Southerners moving into the region, coupled with family tendencies to overcommit, leaves church optional.
ETHNOGRAPHIC PROFILE	Millennials seeking and sacrificing financially, often in a traditional family structure (predominately single), aspiring to succeed in the entertainment and art culture of Hollywood.	People often relocated due to work with three Fortune 200 companies; driven by Walmart; seeking success and quality of life; giving a lot and expecting a lot in return.

NEXT STEPS

After a time for prayer and reflection, write out your own ethnographic profile. Using the template above, work to understand the people you are seeking to reach. Once you have a defined radius for your target audience, consult with your chamber of commerce, civic leaders, and new citizens, both churched and unchurched. Most of all, listen to and examine the feelings and struggles of the unchurched. Develop a determination to respond to these felt needs.

SEVEN

FROM HERDING TO MOBILIZATION

Learning the New Math

MARK GALLI, EDITOR OF *CHRISTIANITY TODAY*, TELLS A STORY OF VISIT-ing a California megachurch. As he talked with the leaders, he learned that the previous night the church had held its first meeting of a new men's ministry. "How did it go?" he asked.

"We had about sixty-six men," replied the minister with a smile. He hadn't had to think about his answer—the answer to how it went was sixty-six. There were no other details or qualifications.

But how were the discussions? What kind of fellowship was shared? How much laughter was heard? In fairness, these things can't be so easily quantified, and the minister simply gave a basic, objective measurement.

Galli recognized surely there weren't "about" sixty-six men. There were *exactly* that many. If it weren't a huge deal, one would have said, "About sixty" or "About seventy"—unless you were taking a precise head count, as this minister surely was.[1]

We keep score in numbers.

We've all been there. In our culture we like measuring things. Bigger is better. Our businesses are run by data, and if we want a raise in salary, we need to show some good numbers—increased sales, more units moved, more sales calls registered.

In the rip-roaring days of the 1980s church growth movement, numbers were at the center of all discussions. How else could you measure the business of reaching people for Christ? Attendance, baptisms, giving, and new buildings. In Christianity we speak of growth physically, mentally, and spiritually, but when we ask someone if his church is growing, they take that to mean *numerically*.

We have to remember the eighties were a go-go decade of business, patriotism, motivation, and goal setting. Not only that, but it was the first wave of the church's response to a perceived crisis. Attendance was plateauing. The Baby Boomers, raised in church, were not returning as young adults. Smaller churches were beginning to vanish like buffalo.

Mainline churches in particular showed the warning signs of extinction, causing evangelicals to pat themselves on the back. Surely, they said, this was an affirmation of conservative doctrine. But many conservative churches were declining too. Southern Baptist growth, long a wonder in ecclesiastical circles, was finally plateauing. Between 2011 and 2012 Baptist membership declined by a startling one hundred thousand—even though there was a greater number of churches.[2] (For more on this decline see chapter 1.)

The church growth movement was built around reversing the frightening trend of numerical decline. Who could complain when new forms of worship broke through, some of the Boomers returned to the strains of contemporary praise music, and new, bulging attendance numbers in certain quarters were celebrated? Most leaders were well versed in the idea that the numbers are important only because *people* are important to us—after all we're in the people business. It's inarguable: being an evangelistic church should eventually show up in the numbers.

Still there was sometimes a feeling of numbers for numbers'

sake. More people. Bigger buildings. Larger budgets. More, more, more. Wasn't it possible for churches to lose their soul in the pursuit of souls in higher volume? The emphasis on numbers eventually gave rise to that emblem of the times: megachurches—sprawling campuses that looked more like shopping malls but offering ministries in place of retail goods. In one well-known megachurch, people were being reached far too quickly to disciple. An excited new believer had an eighteen-month wait to get into a discipleship group.

To its credit the church turned its serious attention toward equipping more leaders to handle those groups. But it was a moment of clarity for church growth. The conversation changed to topics not measured by simple charts: what discipleship means, how to engage members in the life of the church, and the use of spiritual gifts.

Megachurches are not the problem. But they're not necessarily the goal, either. If growth becomes an idol, compromises will inevitably be made. Tell the people what they want to hear, and do it attractively enough, and you're guaranteed to draw crowds. There are massive congregations built on the blandest doctrines of positive thinking, worshiptainment, and self-absorption. At that point, is this a successful church or another Tower of Babel with a coffee shop?

There's a Russian fable about a priest walking down the road to St. Petersburg. A soldier blocks his path and says, "Halt! Who are you? Where are you going? Why are you going there?"

The priest steps back, startled. He pauses a minute and then says, "Sir, I will pay you a worthy sum if you'll wait here once every week, when I pass this way, and ask me those very questions."

We need to ask ourselves those questions:

Who are we?

Where are we going?

Why are we going there?

We might just conclude that we have no idea why we're on a particular road. It just seemed like the cool thing to do according to the last conference we attended. And it might be time to look at the map again. Is gathering the largest crowd in town really the place we most want to go? If we're merely counting sheep, we've dozed off on the job. *Moving* sheep is the mission.

This is why in church, in these times, the new math isn't about how many people you can get under one roof; it's about how many you can mobilize and how effectively they can do kingdom work.

A NEW SCOREBOARD

Many churches have adopted a businesslike matrix for success simply by measuring who they bring into their seats. At our church we like to say that businesses measure success by what they bring in; we measure it by whom we send out. We're concerned with cultivating and equipping people toward an end goal of mobilization. Jesus didn't consider his work done once he reached his disciples. He taught them, trained them, and sent them on a mission.

Our people can be mobilized within the church, toward starting a new church, or for living internationally and doing the work of the kingdom of God.

Attractional ministry, as an end in itself, develops a focus on numbers. It envisions a happy, packed worship center with standing room only. Mission accomplished.

Incarnational ministry—our goal—develops a focus on the work God wants done. It envisions more than a few empty seats, because people are out there with their sleeves rolled up, showing the world what Jesus is like. And the mission is never accomplished until the Master comes back to say so.

We're about so much more than ninety minutes of worship together once per week. Our people aren't seat fillers; they're God's front line, created to do a good work so the "manifold wisdom of God might now be made known to the rulers and authorities in the heavenly places" (Eph. 3:10).

But don't get the idea that we neglect worship or spiritual formation. It's our charge to see our people "to mature manhood, to the measure of the stature of the fullness of Christ" (Eph. 4:13). The most important words in that verse are *mature* and *measure.*

How do we measure maturity? We've tended to do that by creating benchmarks, such as baptism totals, new member classes, variety of programs offered, and fullness of church calendars. I was taught early on to pay close attention to the four Bs: buildings, budgets, baptisms, and butts. And again we find ourselves counting, evaluating things by how they stack up.

Reggie McNeal's book *Missional Renaissance* brings us back to a better matrix, closer to the goals of Ephesians 4:13. He suggested that each church should have its own unique scorecard to reflect its spiritual values. Where your treasure is, there your measure is, you might say—if you value it, count it. He used a resource allocation model to show a change from measuring programs to measuring growth in people. Leaders have to figure out new ways to measure prayer, people, calendars, finances, facilities, and technology, for example.

This is a part of changing the culture by changing the conversation. In the long run you don't want to hear your members say, "We run about a thousand in worship," but rather, "We have seventeen different kinds of ministry stations around the city."[3]

Language needs to be intentional when we want to see change, because what people hear guides how they speak within the same culture, and how they speak ultimately shapes how they think. If we want missions to not be a program but a way of life, as McNeal puts it, we have to paint that picture from every angle, over and over until people begin reflexively to see the picture in their minds. Then we'll have created a missional culture.

Every organization, every culture has a scorecard, however written or spelled out or implied. We grasp it and then reflect it even when we don't realize we're doing so. Therefore, if we value the idea of sending servants into the community and people to the nations, we need to celebrate every score. If we value people pushing toward a deeper prayer life, we need to put it on the scoreboard. There should be faith stories told in church by members who have made breakthroughs in prayer life. Days of sobriety? Celebrate with these people. Members listen and realize this is what the church is about, because you've celebrated it.

Is our church deeply interested in marriages restored to health? Families freed from the bondage of financial debt? Maybe we've been trained to think of these as private matters, but there are still ways to demonstrate these things rather than buildings and attendance totals alone. As pastors plan and write sermons, they should always be conscious that they are the most prominent and powerful voice of their church, and therefore in illustrations and asides, they should be pointing whenever possible to a scorecard that tells what matters to their people.

Numbers have their place. How many classes has the church organized to prepare for international volunteer work? How many people will do short-term missions this year? How many will make long-term commitments to ministry outside the church? Milestones (such as the fifth church we've helped plant) can be commemorated. We simply need to make sure we're finding ways to reflect the heart of an Incarnational Church. We must honor what we value.

Our Resurgent Church is committed to investing in people—in time, in finance, or whatever might be appropriate—so we may one day launch them into their highest calling, their best use of their spiritual gifts, and their deepest service to the kingdom of God.

You don't make disciples out of churches; you make churches out of disciples. Start with discipling and out of that comes a community of believers.

—EDDIE GIBBS[4]

RAISING THE BAR AT MOSAIC

Throughout this book we have returned to the examples of Incarnational Churches that are proving the kingdom of God can be resurgent in this society. Listen to Erwin McManus, lead pastor at Mosaic Church in Los Angeles, as he lamented the choices of the contemporary church:

> We have chosen standardization over uniqueness. We have chosen predictability over surprise. And without realizing it, to our own regret, we have chosen comfort and convenience over servanthood and sacrifice. But in the end, what we have chosen is organization over life, and this, perhaps, is the fundamental dilemma we face—that at best the church is seen as a healthy organization.[5]

McManus is determined that his church won't settle for this brand of cultural mediocrity. Membership at Mosaic is all about *movement* and measurements of it. It's impossible to think of the church as a building or a facility, because it is typified instead by people in motion. Would-be country-club types need not apply.

There are no grandstands for spectators, because the church attempts to be a great playing field with everyone on the team. How is that done? For one thing, leadership distinctions have been blurred or even obliterated. Those who were once called members are now called *staff.* Again, changing the conversation transforms the behavior.

On your first visit to the church, you're told that you're part of the Mosaic community. And once you're interested in joining, the old paradigm of church membership never comes up. Everyone who agrees to be staff understands they have a job description. To be on staff (or volunteer staff, as they like to call it) means:

- I've professed Christ.
- I've been baptized as an informed adult.
- I've completed a Life in Christ spiritual formation journey.
- I've committed 10 percent of my income to the ministry of my church.
- I've been commissioned before the church.

The bar has been raised for going to Mosaic. Volunteer staff are willing to invest their passions (falling in love with Jesus), their relationships (everyone in their circle of influence is an evangelist), their resources (tithing), and their talents (in a meaningful church ministry). These aren't broad guidelines; those not willing to live at this level of commitment don't retain the designation of volunteer staff.

We tend to perceive we get what we pay for. When something is handed out for free, it is devalued in our eyes. The problem with traditional church membership is that it tends to be a giveaway with no strings attached: "Add to our membership numbers by joining us, and we won't bother you about anything else. No one will even notice if you drop out." Given this perception—never spoken but nevertheless communicated—we shouldn't be surprised when people gradually lose interest in church. At the gym, on the other hand, people get a monthly bill; they've pulled out their credit cards and laid them on the altar. If they don't get their money's worth, that's an issue with which they'll contend.

At some point churches accepted the crazy idea that membership isn't easy enough. We didn't use enough grease to slide people down the aisle. I suggest that just the reverse is true—we've asked far too little for far too long.

It makes people feel good to give deeply of themselves (however the transaction works), to receive something deeply new and important to them. The first time you mowed a lawn or babysat for the neighbors, the payment wasn't half as treasured as the feeling of accomplishment. We like to be challenged and to prove ourselves. This is why sports and games have such a powerful appeal. Things have tangible value to the extent we've invested in them.

What does that mean for being part of the church? Membership doesn't need to have its privileges, but it needs to have its price. Set the bar higher. Increase expectations.

Jesus placed a price on following him (Luke 9:23). He talked about a man who found a treasure in a field. He went and sold all he had to buy that field (Matt. 13:44). His treasure followed his heart. Shouldn't we be asking people to give up their small ambitions and join us in an adventure—one that will cost them something but give them everything?

Like Mosaic we want to say, "Jesus wants it all. He wants your relationships. He wants your commitment. He wants your talents and your hard, sweaty work. Are you man enough or woman enough for that challenge?"

THE COST OF COMMITMENT

The Summit Church in Raleigh-Durham, North Carolina, is set in the midst of an academic oasis. Highly educated, tech-savvy young adults are flocking there to build their lives. There are 116,000 college students nearby, and about 1 percent of them are affiliated with one of the Summit Church's nine campuses. These students have all the energy of their youth, and their schedules are crammed to capacity with activities and extra interests. But Pastor J. D. Greear doesn't shy away from asking for a strong mission commitment. It's not *whether* you're called, he tells them, but *where*—so come on, let's find where!

The Summit Church challenges students: give us one summer and two years. That is, one summer of service in and through the church, and two years of career work on mission. Greear wryly calls it his Mormonization strategy, after that church's famous aptitude for required international mission assignments. So far the church has commissioned and sent out 650. Whenever a new believer is baptized, two questions are asked:

1. Are you willing to do whatever God wants you to do?
2. Are you willing to go wherever God wants you to go?

In northwest Arkansas at Grace Point Church, we require a two-day commitment seminar, ending in a final commitment to move from consumer to contributor, attender to member, observer to minister. We challenge people and ask for big things. What if someone says no, they're not willing to explore a ministry position within the church? We can't accept them into membership. We're kind and encouraging, urging them to continue in attendance and prayer until they're ready to take the next step.

Should couples think, pray, and count the cost before marriage? Of course. Should believers do anything less before becoming the bride of Christ?

A good salesman must believe in what he sells. The fact is, we're advocates for Christ. Do we believe in the person and the life we're preaching enough to demand the highest price? Or are we insecure about what we're offering and expecting people to say no?

Jesus talked to a young man—a well-off one—and made the

challenge. It's true, the young man didn't take it. But Jesus met many others who did. He never said, "I want to give you something easy, free, hassleless." Instead, he said, "Take up your cross and follow me." And people did it. They followed him into adventure, surprise, transformation, joy, miracles, and no small amount of pain and occasionally death.

He walked through the margins of society and, without being selective, came across people willing to trade all they had and all they could ever have for a new and vastly greater dream.

Do you think people today are any different? Any less yearning for a life like that?

We need to discard easy, no-hassle membership and challenge people to find out who they can be by how much of themselves they're willing to trade for it.

So much of what we say in church—carefully, inoffensively phrased, polished to a high sheen—goes in one ear and out the other. At the other end of their yawns, the hearers have already forgotten what was said. But look people in the eye, challenge them to trade in their broken aspirations for a new creation, for the service of the King, and their eyes will open wide. They will feel more awake than they've ever been for a long time.

Throughout the week those words will course through their spirit. And they'll be on their way toward mobilization for God's kingdom.

NEXT STEP: 5

- Write your score on your core values as you perceive it honestly, then write a second one for how you wish it was. Gather a diverse group of established members and new members or attenders and ask them what your church values. Compare your list to theirs.

- Spend some time with the church leadership to begin to assess and adjust what it will take to move from herding to mobilizing, if that is one of your values.
- Write two to three clear measurables that will indicate when you are accomplishing your core values.

PROFILE: SARA WILLIAMS

DON AND SARA WILLIAMS HAD NO INTEREST IN FAITH UNTIL THEIR marriage began to crumble. They saw church as a last-ditch attempt to save their relationship. Since we had designed our worship service for de-churched people like the Williamses, they fit in.

As sometimes happens with couples, one was more hesitant than the other. Sara was soon ready to jump in with both feet; Don wanted to take things slowly.

Sara met Lori, my wife, who led her through a Bible study experience. Lori still remembers Sara's joy when she reached a personal milestone—her first experience praying out loud. For you or me, no big deal; for her, a moment full of meaning and promise. That's a scorecard moment to measure.

Sara, who had been in a dark place, was ready to raise the bar of her commitment almost without being asked. She volunteered to work with women, serving as a passionate voice of welcome to those who, like her, were new and didn't know what to expect. "I've been there," she told them. "You're going to love it here." Her engagement was another marker moment—showing her moving forward and outward in her faith.

Then Lori and Sara raised the bar again. They took on a global adventure in Zambia. Like Lori, Sara had traveled extensively. But doing so as an ambassador of Christ was a whole new dimension of life for her. Yet another scorecard moment, and again her faith deepened. Missions touched her in a way nothing else did.

Fifteen times she traveled to West Africa, where she taught the Bible under a mango tree. When back home she found herself looking for ways to increase her ministry overseas. She loved giving herself for mission causes. Sara's career was in the merchandise supply field. One day she had the brainstorm: in an Internet-driven world, she could do her job from anywhere. So she boarded a plane again. By day she was a missionary for Christ; by night she took care of her work.

Grace Point commissioned Sara as our West Africa strategist, and she mobilized more than 130 members to West Africa over a six-year period. It was there that the bar was raised one more time. She spent her last healthy days on a four-month stint in West Africa, teaching young Muslims how to speak English using Mark's gospel as her textbook. She went home to be with her heavenly Father after a bout with cancer. Her funeral was a time of celebration and worship in multiple languages on multiple continents because of all that her life signified to those of us who knew her story.

Don traveled on a few overseas trips, but he understood he really thrived at home in the preschool, teaching four- and five-year-olds. Sara and Don saw their marriage restored and renewed; their faith moved them beyond their seats into action. Grace Point didn't measure their success simply when they joined but when their marriage was restored, and they learned to pray, serve, teach, and go.

So many things move me about the story of Sara and Don, but perhaps the best lesson is the connection between community reach and global reach. When we challenge people to dream big and give the greatest gift possible, they often end up doing that on the widest field possible. All of us for all the world.

EIGHT

FROM COMMUNITY TO COMMUNITAS

Penetrating the Social Matrix

MIT PROFESSOR SHERRY TURKLE SUMMARIZED A FIFTEEN-YEAR STUDY OF the social effects of plugged-in lives in a book titled *Alone Together: Why We Expect More from Technology and Less from Each Other.*[1] She said that we spend time on e-mail, Twitter, Facebook, and other forms of social media thinking that enough sips of real conversation will add up to a generous gulp of deep connection. Ten-word status updates. Quick tweets about restaurant destinations. Just a few words at a time, but we do it frequently, meaning a whole lot of a tiny little.

Of course we find that communication doesn't work like a water fountain. Sips don't have a cumulative effect. Our connections are globally wide and an eighth of an inch deep. At the end of the day, it only accentuates our loneliness. You can't have a meaningful exchange in Twitter's 140-character limit. We need just a few real characters in our lives, and we need soul-depth.

Turkle observed that our gadgets, always on and always on us, provide the illusion of being with others. And we notice that when people are physically alone, even for a moment, they begin to fidget, reach for their phones, and check for messages even though they did that five minutes ago. How many times a day do we see that in public? It's the enduring image of these times, and it means more than we think.[2] People need connections that even the widest mobile network can't reach. They need community.

A recent study was based on a random selection of three thousand people with the goal of finding out how connected they are. Average Americans, it was discovered, have only four close social contacts.[3] Again the irony is inescapable. We're told only six degrees of separation exist between anyone in the world and us. Connection is perhaps the greatest technological marvel of these times, and yet we've forgotten how to connect in a way that nourishes the soul.

Social media is the hit of the last decade or so. It has changed culture more than anything since the Internet itself. Experts are only beginning to understand the seismic changes this phenomenon has brought to our world. Social media has toppled nations (for example, the 2010 Arab Spring), impacted presidential elections, created marriage matches, and destroyed some of the same marriages. A counselor told me that abuse of social media is a common factor in marriages destroyed by infidelity.

It's easy to curse the darkness, but let's not overlook the need to light a candle where appropriate. Spiritual issues, for instance, can be discussed or at least sparked in new ways through social media. Missionaries can go to places where passports are unavailable. Bible studies occur in real time between people in several different nations, all chatting over Facebook or in a chat room.[4] Like everything else, new technology is neither divine nor demonic; it's a neutral vessel that we must decide how to use.

But we would be naive not to recognize that social media is changing us in ways we can't completely comprehend. Families, marriages, careers, politics, friendships. There seems to be no corner of public or private life social media can't penetrate—other than the deepest needs of the human soul. Therefore we must be as wise as serpents and as gentle as doves in devising our use of it.

What about church? Community is a different entity now. Since the inception of the body of Christ, community occurred in physical space, generally inside a building. "For where two or three are gathered in my name, there am I among them," Jesus promised in Matthew 18:20. Who said we had to share the same location?

Technology has afforded us new ways for two or more to gather. We can, in fact, connect online in coffee shops, at pubs, and in yoga studios. (Yoga studios? Yes! Where better to bring the gospel than to a place connected to Eastern religions?)

Social media can be just another trap or it can be just another tool. But there's a third possibility. It can provide a convenient snapshot of the state of our culture. It can be a light into the longing of our souls. I was recently on a flight and noticed how a Millennial used her time waiting for takeoff. Social media owned every second until the wheels were up and the Wi-Fi was taken away. At that point she opened a photograph and began editing it. We were up in the air for an hour, and she gave all sixty minutes to editing that photo. It was going to be a small masterpiece: tint, contrast, filters, features. Then, as soon as the wheels hit the ground, she uploaded her new, improved photo to social media.

We can't watch a scene like this, or countless others you're likely to see out and about, without asking what can be learned about the longings of our souls. If, as Jesus said, the heart is to be found where our treasures are (Matt. 6:21), we need to understand how the conception of treasure has changed in these times. Social media, with its enormous success, is a series of Rorschach drawings that speak to the psychology of our times.

New venues come and go quickly in the technoverse, but as I write, four giants stand above the rest: Facebook, Instagram,

Twitter, and LinkedIn. Why? To answer that question is to find telling clues about this soul hunger. We want to learn what the social media explosion tells us about people and use that information to help us reach the people so captivated by it.

The four giants each reveal something about these times and these people.

FACEBOOK: CONTINUOUS ORGANIC COMMUNITY

Friended used to be merely an example of bad grammar. Now it's a concept that has redefined relationships across the world. Facebook has made 24/7 companionship possible.

Yes, it's shallow and carefully framed. We see closely sculpted glimpses of people rather than honest portrayals, making every user his own PR specialist. Photos are edited to remove wrinkles, and status updates are full of happy talk, constantly offering the message, "Isn't it great to be me?" If each were true, earth would be heaven.

On the other hand Facebook has helped countless people reconnect, from old summer camp buddies to high school sweethearts. Reunions among all kinds of forgotten groups, cliques, and organizations became a phenomenon after Facebook took off. It's hard not to think of this as a positive thing. Also many found ways to be encouragers through Facebook, and they could do so far and wide. Missionaries no longer had to run up long-distance bills while speaking only to loved ones; now an entire church can follow their daily victories and setbacks through a Facebook page.

People can call out for a community of prayer quickly and effectively. I have counseled old friends from high school, connected with ex-cons, and interact nearly every Sunday morning with a national church planter in West Africa through Facebook. We pray and encourage each other as he ends his day and I start mine.

This site can be a pit of vanity and self-promotion or a significant place of service to humanity—it's up to the user. As in everything else in life, what we build from raw materials speaks volumes about who we are. But the most powerful message is this: we were created for community. We delight in connecting with others, even if it's through the dubious realities of cyberspace. We were made for a togetherness that ultimately reflects the perfect communion of the Godhead, and a perfect union calls out to us. A new way of making that happen was sure to be an international phenomenon.

What should this say to the Resurgent Church? We teach our children the little song, "The church is not a building—the church is people." J. D. Greear of the Summit Church in Raleigh-Durham, however, says that church isn't even people; it's something that *happens*. It's a supernatural event. Otherwise it's no different than the Rotary Club. Just as the noun *Facebook* has become a verb for some ("I was Facebooking last night"), so we should think of church as something we do rather than a roll call pictured by the church directory. We do our relationships through the power of the body of Christ, and we're having church.

Furthermore Greear and his staff have instilled into their culture the idea that *discipleship happens in relationship.* Because of Facebook's private groups feature, you can take advantage of small group accountability anytime you are connected to Wi-Fi. If we look to programs to accomplish that, we'll miss the mark. Programs are helpful only insofar as they spark relationships, and clearly the best program for sparking relationships is the small group. Every Resurgent Church I've studied agrees on the primacy of small groups. Having small groups wasn't enough; small groups that foster community are the true goal.

Mosaic, meanwhile, has simple goals for its groups: share life together through Scripture. Former small groups directional pastor Chad Becker observed that these groups should reflect life itself— at times very structural, at times messy, but always as fulfilling as personal connection allows. In this Facebook society, we understand the meaning of that.

> Postmodern ministry must contend with the strong sense of ownership people feel with Facebook. We want to be known. We want our thoughts, opinions, and passions to be heard. What kind of forums can the church create for people to express their hopes and hunger, to share their glee and mark signposts along their journeys?
>
> —CRAIG DETWEILER[5]

INSTAGRAM: EPIC MOMENTS CAPTURED IN IMAGE

Launched as recently as 2010, Instagram understands the power of imagery to tell a story. For every short-form wordsmith laboring over a status update on Facebook, there is a visual learner who believes a picture is worth a thousand words. And from what we know about these times, that user may be on to something.

The postmodern era is all about imagery and the power of what we see. Jacques Ellul's *Humiliation of the Word*[6] explores the dangers of image media displacing word media. There are still many times when pictures fall short and we need to use our words.

Still, we must understand that written-word-oriented people are far harder to come by these days. Twenty-five years ago you might have told a nonbelieving friend, "I have a great book by C. S. Lewis that deals with these spiritual questions. Can I loan it to you?" Today you might be greeted with a look of horror. "You want me to *read a book*?" Nearly every guy we meet is a man of few words, it seems. At least when it comes to getting a text from them.

If you're reading these words in book form (rather than waiting for the author to make it more palatable on YouTube or feed it to you in bright PowerPoint colors)—congratulations! You're truly retro. But you need to understand our culture is moving in a different direction.

That's a challenge. Our faith is logical, detailed, based upon written history, and empowered by a theology that needs to be expounded in words and theoretical ideas. At some point, people need to read the New Testament or they simply won't get it. But our challenge today is to find better ways to be visual in our presentations.

Darrell Bock of Dallas Theological Seminary, a respected professor of New Testament studies, told me about changes he has seen in his students. Getting students to read is a deep struggle. Steep text assignments are almost painful to them. He believes they've been so stimulated and overstimulated by various lively media that their capacity to focus has been compromised.

I asked him how a professor can possibly stimulate effective learning in such an environment. "We have to be creative," he said. Podcasts. Video. Use technology familiar to your students.

We can't afford to dumb anything down. But I believe these situations give birth to new, creative approaches. Nothing is new under the sun. There is no problem that God's Spirit won't crack. In the Middle Ages, cathedrals were giant Bibles. Walk through Chartres Cathedral in France and you see the whole story of the Old and New Testaments depicted in stained-glass windows for a medieval society of largely illiterate people. Images still tell stories of times, places, and people that mean something to us. Instagram has given individuals their own cathedral to enshrine their own life moments—even if most of these are selfies. Words are not the only way.

Another huge Instagram lesson is that life is now perceived as a collection of moments. The celebration of ordinary moments is commonplace now—something that wouldn't have occurred to people in the past. "Here's our group at the game." "Look who I ran into at lunch!"

We need to build powerful moments filled with meaning for people—with or without ubiquitous camera phones. And there are wonderful and significant ways of doing it, as long as we do it for the right reasons and not just to have a moment. Like life a moment is something that happens while you're making other plans. At the Summit Church there is an understanding that small groups will get out of living rooms and into community action. The goal is to connect every group with a local outreach ministry. The members may feel called to prison ministry, helping unwed mothers-to-be, or tutoring in schools. When we're doing it right, the result will be epic moments that create image-rich experiences that ignite faith and transformation in lives. Is your small group creating moments that are photoworthy?

It's not important that Instagram moments result but that true community and gospel moments occur. In this transient society, people come into our fellowship and then leave it with rapidity. "We post pictures of events as they happen because we have no time to pause or reflect. Instagram is a way to externalize what used to be an interior activity."[7] As in the title of Eugene Peterson's book *A Long Slow Obedience in the Same Direction,*[8] long and slow obedience is the ideal, but we also have to take advantage of the swatches of time that people may give us during their ceaseless, nomadic life journeys.

A truly passionate Resurgent Church will build a variety of symbolic, memorable, and visually rich moments.

—————————— SHOW ME ——————————

Recently the *Chicago Tribune* instituted a major redesign to be more image- and web-friendly. This included eliminating half their staff, mostly writers.

We may moan about this, but it tells us yet again that the written word in our society is no longer the dominant mode of communication. Visual media—pictures, film, video, symbols, logos, icons, emoticons—are winning the day.[9]

TWITTER: INTENTIONAL AND TO-THE-POINT COMMUNICATION

If Facebook captures the craving for community and Instagram is about visual moments, then Twitter is for a culture that wants to live in a headlong rush while missing nothing.

Twitter is the Internet's answer to the "continuous partial attention"[10] of this generation. Twitter is about brevity, pragmatism, and mobility. If you want to say it, you have to get it done in 140 characters—a sentence or perhaps two short ones, often including a hyperlink and seeking retweets. The unspoken goal is building followers (digital disciples). Pew Research pointed out that 61 percent of Millennials (nineteen- to thirty-four-year-olds) get their news via social media, which tends to be more opinion-based.[11] We are a culture of edited sound bites. Barack Obama was the first American president to capitalize on using Twitter for his election run.

The cofounder of Twitter, Jack Dorsey, told the *Los Angeles Times*: "Bird chirps sound meaningless to us, but meaning is applied by other birds. The same is true of Twitter: a lot of messages can be seen as completely useless and meaningless, but it's entirely dependent on the recipient."[12] Beyond the distorted marketing schemes, in which you may follow thousands of people while reading none of them, the ideal is that you follow and listen, favorite, or even retweet the statements of people you are truly reading.

Half a billion people use Twitter, though it can be puzzling at first. An incredible wealth of information flows through the Internet in those quick, terse lines. The message itself may be compact, but an effective one (judged by its retweets) is the result of careful consideration and creativity—maximization of limited length.

What if small groups gathered around affinities or tribes of like-minded people? Grace Point Church has artist tribes that gather for community, CrossFitter groups, and even a group of people with a passion to teach preschoolers. One group gathers as a support group because all the members are parents of teenagers. Woven into their intentional meetings is the ideal of helping parents at a particular stage sort things out. These are the tribes of the Twitter generation.

Chad Becker, former small groups pastor at Mosaic, found ways to pack a lot of truth in a small, creative package. One small group has question and response times with about seventy participants. People bring their questions and break into smaller groups to discuss them. Mosaic also uses book clubs geared around new releases by Erwin McManus, the lead pastor. *The Artisan Soul: Crafting Your Life into a Work of Art*[13] was the subject of recent discussions.

Like Twitter the slant was short, highly focused, and pragmatic. While there are normally perhaps 80 small groups, the church found it could launch 350 limited-period, tight-subject book clubs in the LA area. Since this context involves younger people in the arts, notice how the topic (developing art in artists) and the approach (short-lived, intentional groups) were perfectly designed for their community. Mosaic understands gospel truth for the Twitter generation.

Some parables of Jesus can be considered first-century tweets (or Instagram pics): the lost pearl, the hidden treasure, the net. So often he linked his teaching to simple, terse imagery and information to point to deeper, more profound truths about God's kingdom. He delivered his truth in quick, creative, and memorable forms that his followers remembered for decades before recording them in the Gospels. Twitter may be new, but teaching abides through all generations.

LINKEDIN: GATHERING AROUND MISSION

Soma Communities, which is committed to incarnational ministry, describes itself as "a smaller group of people who gather regularly and engage in everyday life on mission throughout the week with a commitment to reaching a particular people and place together with the goal of making disciples and multiplying and sending more."[14] That also expresses what LinkedIn is all about.

It was inevitable that the principles of social media would find form in the marketplace. LinkedIn continues to grow in influence among a transient world of career people. In the United States alone, one hundred million users network through the site.

Users of LinkedIn focus on what they do, how well they do it, and where they do it. They have a place to sell themselves and to receive endorsements from others, with the understanding that they'll return the favor. This friend is good at this; that friend is good at that.

We're reminded in LinkedIn that we're all ultimately connected, all part of one global family. LinkedIn creates a network that helps people reach out to others and build virtual connections that could possibly grow into true relationships through hiring or partnering together in some work project. As the church we're reminded of the countless links we share with those in the world. Within our fellowship we connect with the body of Christ. And yet we realize our tenuous links to all kinds of people who cross our paths, and each of these links is a mission potentiality. LinkedIn is constantly prodding users: Do you know this person? Can you rate this one? And we find ourselves looking for new connections. Is this not the reflection of a church on mission to its community, looking all the time for links, new community bonds, and new opportunities for engagement?

The Next Church—the Resurgent Church—must not only know the cutting edge of its culture, but it must see to the heart of its context. As we do so, we realize what we have to offer is infinitely more powerful, truer, and more fulfilling than any mere form of technology or the connection it could offer. We can offer real community and something deeper still. The church, at its best, makes possible what sociologists call *communitas*.

COMMUNITAS

Communitas is a heightened sense of community. Over and beyond most of what we think of as community in a church—typical, comfortable fellowship—*communitas* is what happens when people forge a tight bond through either crisis or a powerful sense of mission. Everyone is working together; no one wears a mask.

In his writings Alan Hirsch pointed to the early Christians and the more recent Chinese Christian underground as situations in which believers, through persecution, experienced liminality (see chapter 2). As a result they found uncommon relationships together, which people around them found irresistible, no matter how dangerous it was to identify with Jesus.[15]

In the church *communitas* expresses itself best in the small group experience. We find that the four components of social media we've discussed that have connected so powerfully with our society can become goals to build our groups around. There is a matrix in which, if we consider these social media forms in tandem, we discover the needs we should be attempting to meet.

For example, Instagram and LinkedIn are about *shaping* us. One gives us epic moments captured in images; the other expresses our talents and skills, careers and passions. Yet when we combine Instagram and Facebook, we see the connection to *relationship*. We follow and friend people we like and want to be like. We want affirmation and give affirmation with a simple Like button. Affirmation builds relationship.

Facebook and Twitter combine to speak to *meaning* in life. Our relationships have a voice. With Twitter's acquisition of Periscope, the new social media video portal, people can stream their ideas and agendas to friends and followers. Life has meaning, and that meaning can be shared.

How do LinkedIn and Twitter interface? The word here is *impact*. We have a voice and a network within a profession. This gives us credibility to speak.

SHAPE

RELATIONSHIP	INSTAGRAM
	Epic moments captured in images
	
	   – Images make
	     time stand still
		LINKEDIN
		Gathering around mission
		
		   – My life has skills
		     and passion
			IMPACT

	FACEBOOK
	Continuous organic community
	
	   – 24/7 relationships
		TWITTER/PERISCOPE
		Communication is trivial to intentional
		
		   –I have a voice in the world	

MEANING

Shape. Relationship. Meaning. Impact. When I think of the small groups in my church, I think of that airline passenger using all her Wi-Fi time on social media, and then using all of her non-Wi-Fi time to edit a picture to later upload on social media. That's an image of craving. How are my church's small groups addressing those cravings? How are we shaping people using skills and gifts? How are we creating true, genuine relationships that immerse people in one another's lives? Where is meaning being discovered?

What sense of impact in the world do these people gain through the matrix of connection they find in that group?

We've got to be more than a little cluster of couples enjoying a supper club. We've got to be more even than a band of spiritual pilgrims exploring God's Word. *Communitas* is a heightened, gospel-level bond of people encountering God and one another as they go on mission.

ON MISSION TOGETHER

During World War II the paratroopers portrayed in Stephen Ambrose's book and miniseries *Band of Brothers*[16] first bonded together at Toccoa, Georgia, near a mountain called Currahee. The men adapted the meaning of the word *currahee* as their motto: "We Stand Alone Together." That captures a bit of what *communitas* is. In foxholes across Belgium near the German border in December 1944, during the Battle of the Bulge, these soldiers experienced incredible, nerve-shattering conditions of unpredictable shellings, inadequate provisions, and freezing temperatures. For decades the survivors spoke about the transcendent sense of togetherness they shared in those trenches. Every man was equal because each was dependent upon the man next to him. Any soldier would give his life for his buddy. They stood alone together: *communitas*.

Like many churches Grace Point seeks to create *communitas* through small group ministry. Smaller groups, meeting casually in living rooms over time, are far more likely to break down social barriers. We refer to it as a community for the community. Comfortable, convenience-centered groups, of course, won't experience what we're looking for, so it's not just enough to find a leader and start a group. What must happen is for a bonded group of believers to begin living everyday life on mission and with incarnational hearts for their community. Yes, their group is sanctuary, a place to learn and grow and encourage, but it is also a point of departure. When they come to understand how the Spirit binds them together, combines their gifts, and helps them to do the supernatural, they experience this heightened level of unity and mutual dependence.

In traditional congregational community, we can meet many of these needs. We can savor deeper relationships; we can encourage and be encouraged; we can simply hang out and help one another navigate the wild rapids of everyday life.

But *communitas*, as we're coming to understand it, reaches deeper. We want to do all those things and do them well. But we also realize that we move from the natural to the supernatural when we serve God together. We go somewhere social media—nor anything else—can't match. There is strength in numbers, there is power in presence, and as we advance into the darkness, courageous in our unity, we become something together that is more than the sum of our parts. It can only be described as *oneness*, and perhaps the only worthy comparison is marriage. As we've said, the ultimate foundation is found in the perfect, transcendent interrelationships between Father, Son, and Holy Spirit. The communion we seek is always a response to our God image, the craving for the perfect union of Three in One.

At our best, we fall a good way's short of experiencing Trinitarian completeness or even the potential of the holy union of marriage. But *communitas* has its own unique aspects of joy and fulfillment. It's unlike any other feeling in life. In *communitas*, we are the church, not in any stale organizational tradition, but in the blueprint drawn up by God for all of time. We join hands with the original apostles and all of those who have followed since. We are the living link to the future and the time when Christ returns—and we feel the power of what God is doing. In *communitas*, our spiritual gifts move into action, and we see our little selves doing mighty things we never thought possible.

Resurgent Churches will be driven and empowered by a deep, transcendent form of togetherness through which we'll divide the darkness like the waters of the Red Sea and let God's light shine to a desperate world.

NEXT STEPS

Evaluate your small group on a scale of one to ten.

1 = not currently   5 = sometimes   10 = all the time

- Is there a 24/7 community feel that we long for on Facebook?
- Are there epic moments to celebrate together that someone organically wants to post?
- Is the communication meaningful, calculated, and intentional?
- Is my group on a mission to do and make an impact?

PROFILE: A COMMUNITY FOR THE COMMUNITY

At some point we looked at one another and faced the truth: in the church culture with which we were familiar, Sunday school had its limits. Classes had turned into not-so-holy huddles where doughnuts, coffee, gossip, and stray bits of gospel were consumed. Would the organization produce new believers? Probably not. Could we drop in new believers and know they'd become fully formed disciples? In most cases, no.

When we birthed Grace Point, we knew we needed something new. Like thousands of other churches, we knew we wanted to do small groups in homes, with Bible study, prayer, fellowship, and—last but by no means least—mission. This wasn't going to be a supper club with a devotional. We wanted people in motion. We wanted northwest Arkansas to figure out quickly that something was going on at our church because our people seemed to be everywhere. And should we vanish for some reason, we wanted people to notice that, too, and regret it deeply.

I could tell many stories of our groups. One of them had a brainstorming session about how to serve the community. One of the members was a deputy sheriff with the county. He cared deeply about men trying to make a new start after being released from jail.

A men's homeless shelter was suggested as a community resource. Why not work with that group? Before long, the group had set up a date for serving meals to some of the men. There was a terrific cookout with big dishes of burgers and side dishes, as well as budding friendships with the men of the shelter. Soon after that, the group also sat down with the director and asked how else they could help. "Funny you should ask," he said. "We're trying to build a new kitchen and dining facility."

So the group was back the next week, this time with hammers, shovels, and some extra manpower. Somebody brought a friend who was a construction pro, and the project went well.

Soon there were other endeavors: fund-raising to rebuild and repair a greenhouse on the property, for example. The group got excited about this, mobilized to raise twelve hundred dollars through a skip-a-meal fund-raising plan—and then the whole church got excited and pitched in to make the total five thousand dollars. (You'll find that an excited group creates a mission infection in your church.) The greenhouse was beautifully restored.

The more the group ministers, the deeper the bond it shares among its members. That's what *communitas* does.

NINE

FROM SHEPHERD TO PIONEER

Entrepreneurial Apostleship

IF YOU WERE GIVEN A TIME MACHINE AND ALLOWED TO USE IT ONCE, where would you go? Many of the more spiritually minded would want to see Jesus and want to be there on that first Easter Sunday. So let's say anything *besides* that.

For me it's a no-brainer. I'd want to visit the first century so I could see the first leaders of the church, watching them grow from mice to men—to men of valor.

The book of Acts already gives us a pretty good picture of how the disciples and those around them worked, but I'd still give a great deal to have a front-row seat for the vision of what the Spirit of God did in and through those ordinary men.

Can you imagine being in the room when Paul, once known as Saul, first met Peter, John, and the others? We know that Peter and Paul spent fifteen days together early in Paul's ministry (Gal. 1:18). I'd love to be a fly on the wall and hear what passed between those two. But here's how I imagine it.

Peter and Paul are talking about Jesus. Paul, of course, is hungry to know what it was like to know and follow the Master in the flesh. Then, inevitably, they turn to the future.

"More and more people are coming to Jerusalem," Peter says. "What an incredible chance we have to tell them about Jesus."

"No doubt," Paul smiles. "But why sit here and wait? What if we *went to them*?"

"What? How would we do that?"

"Just go where the people are. The Romans have built incredible roads—these new ships are seaworthy. People speak Greek everywhere! Why not divide up and go tell them about Jesus?"

"Because—because this is Jerusalem. The church is here! Because it's, well, it's the new temple, right? People have always come here to worship God."

"So there can only ever be one church? And people have to come here to be in it? Might get crowded. And didn't you tell me the last thing Jesus said was—"

"But this is where all the Jews are!"

"Think big, Peter. Isn't Jesus for everybody? We should be on the *move*. 'The ends of the earth' are a pretty good way from Jerusalem."

What a conversation it must have been. Peter, a courageous, bold, and empowered apostle by this time—but not a creative one. Still, he was a born entrepreneur. He knew his goal, he understood the great cultural changes around him, and he adapted to reach his goal in the midst of those changes, always at great risk.

Men like Peter provide the *sturdy leadership* upon which we build. Men like Paul provide the *fluid creativity* that makes all the right moves at precisely the right times.

God has always called powerful entrepreneurs at critical points of time. Martin Luther's powerful biblical ideas about justification by faith spread like wildfire because of a brand-new invention: the printing press.

John Wesley, at the outset of the Industrial Revolution, was a powerful social entrepreneur. His credo—"Make all you can, save all you can, give all you can"—was an empowering idea for the growing business class. The Guinness family, known for brewing, were so influenced by his preaching that Arthur Guinness began channeling his wealth into starting urban Sunday schools and hospitals for the poor—an early model of incarnational ministry in the city.[1]

As a matter of fact, many evangelical practices we take for granted today, such as the altar call and walking the aisle, come from the time of Wesley, when circuit riders on horseback would cover thousands of miles of American wilderness. Since they might not come that way again for some time, they realized the need to be intentional about requesting a decision for Christ then and there. Such a thing had never been part of their Anglican roots, but the American prairie called for new and different approaches. Creative responses to those approaches gave birth to such modern denominations as Southern Baptists and Methodists.

These leaders recognized changes in society, and they focused on how the gospel interfaced with those changes (as it always will). As a result, the church rode each new wave of social revolution like an expert surfer.

Instead of change being a threat, it becomes an open door to new, revitalizing opportunities for the people of God. A crashing wave on the seashore is an act of God. Some see it as a disaster, others as the chance for a high-water mark.

THE SHEPHERD NEEDS NEW SKILLS

The enduring metaphor of the spiritual leader is that of the shepherd. It's an image older than Christianity—embedded in the very identity of Old Testament Israel and its relationship to God. In an agriculturally based world, everyone understood the idea of the field hand responsible for the flock. Psalm 23 depicted God as the Good Shepherd, and Jesus called himself "the good shepherd" (John 10:11).

But every analogy has its limits, even the deepest and most biblical of them. The shepherd focuses on care and nurture; the spiritual metaphor works best when the church needs only do the same. In the much more closed culture of ancient Israel—or, say, colonial Plymouth—*shepherd* was the right word. Within Christendom, a pastor could be looked upon as the appointed caretaker of the flock. The shepherd wasn't required to go out and *recruit* the sheep; they were assigned to him. Don't hear me say that caring for the flock isn't important; even in a day of gospel advancement, pastoral care was in place (Acts 20:25–31). But new days call for new skills not commonly developed in pastors.

Post-Christendom changes everything about those conditions. The shepherd now becomes a rescuer. We could, of course, reference the parable of Jesus in which the shepherd leaves the ninety-nine to seek out the one straggler (Luke 15:3–6). But again, the lost sheep is somewhat of an exception. In our current world it's far from a single lamb out there in the wilds. The lost ones are all across the landscape, and the shepherd is going to have a sense of urgency about that. Wolves are about!

Now he needs to be clever, not just tender. He realizes he must have an expert grasp of the terrain around him, and he needs to be very quick and efficient in his rescue missions.

That's when the shepherd realizes he needs a few new tools. He needs to be an *entrepreneur of gathering* as well as caring for sheep. That is, the shepherding part must continue. Sheep, like people, must always be cared for. But the total job description must change. The shepherd realizes he is in a new world, where the rugged and treacherous terrain is constantly shifting. The wolves this week may look very different next week.

The entrepreneurial church leader, too, must know the culture around him. He must be a creative and clever thinker; he must have the tools for responding or know where to find them; and he must be utterly proactive and aggressive in the approach to ministry in this setting.

We speak of entrepreneurs, but it's not our first go-around with business models. In the age of the megachurch (which is ongoing), it was the CEO that originally seemed like the best pastoral model. Church leadership manuals of the eighties and nineties often looked to the boardroom of Fortune 500 companies for guidance. How would FedEx approach this church? What can Apple or Jack Welch teach me about management vision? Like the shepherd, the CEO leaned upon his staff, although his was composed of middle managers rather than birch.

Now we know, however, that being a good corporate manager isn't enough. Overseeing a staff of deacons and specialized professional ministers is meaningless if nobody on the team has a clue as to how to share the gospel to an uncomprehending and seemingly uninterested world. And the ideas of vision—usually translated as larger attendance and more impressive facilities—are empty once we realize we're still losing ground in the world.

"Build it and they will come" no longer counts as a mission statement. We know now that we need an approach more visionary, more radical, more intelligently centered in the people we yearn to reach—and we need the genuine supernatural power of Christ rather than fancy buildings and programs. We need the bold, wise, creative spirit of the entrepreneur.

At this point as we see the need for significant changes in the traditional leadership profile, it's fair to ask whether our seminaries are already working toward this level of transition. (For the record, many of them are.) What kinds of courses need to be initiated? What departments need to be founded? Where will we find qualified professors who can prepare the next generation of leaders? Denominations and independent Bible schools and seminaries can't afford to delay in asking these questions.

Even so we suspect the best work—by definition—will come from the least theologically trained, at least formally. Just as the greatest business innovators never attended big business schools, the true entrepreneurs will be laypeople who haven't been programmed to think inside the old boxes.

THE RETURN OF THE APOSTLE

I'm not here to suggest this form of leadership is something to consider for the future; I'm here to confirm that it's already on the job.

In my study of resurgent, growing churches with incarnational ministry, the most frequent of all the shared traits is that these churches had clear entrepreneurial leadership. Members and ministry leaders of the Summit Church, Mosaic Church, and others agreed, almost at a unanimous level, that their pastor has a clear and compelling vision for the direction of their church.

This has been true particularly over the last decade or so. The churches that are positively and powerfully impacting their communities in the post-Christendom world are led by creative, innovative change agents who have decided exactly where they're going. And they are building new kinds of structures and writing new rules to get them there.

Among those studying these trends, the word *entrepreneur* is seen frequently, along with another interesting descriptor: *apostle.* This is the word that makes the connection from the business terminology to its congregational application, thus linking first-century to twenty-first century ministry. The entrepreneurial spirit in Resurgent Churches is often described as *apostolic.*

Rigidly defined the word *apostle* is limited to first-generation followers who actually saw Jesus, namely, the Twelve plus Paul. But we're using the word in a more general sense today to describe the special, dynamic creativity and spirit of courageous calling exemplified by those early disciples. Alan Hirsch has talked about apostolic genius, a powerful and uniquely Christian force that pervades explosive ministries and churches. He unpacks this concept in detail in his book titled *The Forgotten Ways: Reactivating the Missional Church*.[2]

We're called not simply to admire what the first-century Christians did, Hirsch says, but to replicate it. After all, Jesus told the Twelve they would perform greater miracles than his. In essence, he is speaking over their shoulders to challenge us. Hirsch believes we can't reach the world in any effective measure within the limits of the preacher-teacher model; we need the apostolic entrepreneur. We can't grow with inward-focused growth groups, but we must exemplify outward-focused *communitas* (see previous chapter).

There is a missional DNA (mDNA) that springs from an absolute passion for the truth that Jesus is Lord. His lordship is our power and spiritual authority, freeing us to bring Christ into any environment, regardless of its challenges and resistance. While Hirsch offers six points of similarity among those explosive churches and movements, he never offers these as steps in a simple formula. Instead, the traits are organic to one another, all part of a brand-new mind-set leaders must own.

Again we think of Paul, the entrepreneurial apostle. He had a profound, highly infectious concept of the lordship of Christ and an arrestingly simple mission statement: "To be a minister of Christ Jesus to the Gentiles" (Rom. 15:16). His power and passion came from the lordship of Christ, and his every action was controlled by that mission statement which took hold of him even as Christ took hold of him.

Because of these things all he did was brand-new—going into marketplaces to preach the gospel, starting new churches in strange and hostile cities, and working through a thousand new problems and questions that had never been raised—simply because he took the new path that his calling demanded. If people had worn T-shirts, his would have said, "Powered by Apostolic Genius."

In Christian history we can find models of entrepreneurship, but few, obviously, from a post-Christendom context. We have to follow the first-century church's lead, but we need to do so in our own modern context. And because of the nature of this—organic, contextual solutions rather than prefab models—the answers will be different for every church. A church in Raleigh-Durham (the Summit Church) responds to a highly academic young community. A church in Los Angeles (Mosaic) responds to a community deeply entrenched in or attracted to the entertainment world. Not all examples will be as singular as these—there will be certain models of ministry that may work in both midtown Atlanta and urban Cleveland. Some of our strategies in northwest Arkansas may be applicable to settings that share many of our cultural traits (though even in our case, the presence of three large corporate cultures makes us unique).

The wrong question is how our hero churches are doing it. The right questions are, What is my community all about? How can *we* do it?

THE MEANING OF ENTREPRENEURIAL

The key word in this chapter has an elusive definition. It's one of those "I can't define it, but I know it when I see it" ideas. Typical definitions speak of starting a new business using innovation and taking risks. But how does it apply in the cultural world of church? Allow me to suggest some of the habits of highly entrepreneurial church leaders.

- **Courageous in attitude.** The CEO model, of course, constantly thinks in terms of stewardship. This can seem to be an argument against risk—protecting the investment as a high priority. Yet the parables of Jesus often suggest Jesus as a manager who expects his stewards to be fruitful rather than burying their investments. When we think of apostles, one of the first words that comes to mind is "courageous," not "careful and thrifty."

- **Visionary in seeing.** Jesus didn't stop with talking about the future but spoke to eternity itself. He lived his whole life in a couple of zip codes, yet he spoke of the ends of the earth. He revered the Law of Moses, yet he saw beyond it to a new and greater law. Visionary leaders never lose sight of the big picture and speak it into permanent residence in the minds of their followers.
- **Strategic in thinking.** The pioneering leader, committed to the picture of a desired future, is already designing the stairway to reach it. As the vision clarifies, the strategies begin to suggest themselves. The entrepreneurial leader instinctively seeks these out, even though he's the "big picture" type.
- **Purpose-centered in action.** The leader looks over his organization and asks, Why are we doing this? If there is anything that makes him crazy, it is wasted motion—defined as energy expended toward a nongoal. He keeps the main thing as the main thing.

MEMO FOR THE PIONEER BEGINNER

We're talking about a powerful leadership profile that looks very different from the churches that we actually see. For most of us it's hard to read, think about, and discuss these needs without feeling some sense of inadequacy. The questions rise up before us:

- What if my personal gifts don't measure up to this new kind of leader?
- How could I ever turn my entrenched deacons and elders in such new and risky directions?
- Where do I even begin?

135

We begin with the promises of God, who assured Moses he would give him the words before Pharaoh, who told Joshua to be strong and courageous, who (in the person of Jesus) told the disciples that his presence and power would follow them to every corner of the earth. The essence of Hirsch's apostolic genius is that Jesus is Lord, and that out of this flows a power from the Spirit of God that has nothing to do with our meager abilities or inabilities.

God always provides a way. Courage and sacrifice will be required, but that's true of anything truly worthwhile in life. And we're speaking of things that are worthwhile in eternity.

Here are some action points for those contemplating a new, more entrepreneurial direction in ministry.

1. Train outside your comfort zone. We like to talk about unprecedented challenges, but what about unprecedented opportunities? The Internet offers access to incredible potential. For example, consider Willow Creek Community Church's Global Leadership Summit, with a wide variety of training and cutting-edge insights. At the 2011 Summit 165,000 leaders from more than 20,000 churches took part remotely from Willow Creek broadcasts. You might also follow the innovation of leadership at sites such as Fast Company (http://www.fastcompany.com/leadership).

2. Read widely and practically. If the last three books you read were straight spiritual, it's time to read more contemporary works on creative leadership. Some of my favorite forward thinkers include Patrick Lencioni, Jim Collins, Seth Godin, and Daniel Pink. Read from the pioneers who have preceded us. Try some missionary biographies, such as Hudson Taylor, William Carey, Bertha Smith, or Jim and Elisabeth Elliot. My favorite is David Livingstone. In other words, read not

only pragmatically but also for inspiration and for recharging your circuits. The pioneers of the past can jump-start the new pioneers.

3. Spend time with change agents. Who do you know who is shaking things up in a positive and productive way? Find out their secrets. You might pay someone in the creative realm to let you shadow them for a day or two, making observations. You'll need to be ready to cover the cost. Then study their disciplines, find out what they're reading, where their inspiration comes from, and ask why—ask why frequently. Do this sensitively and respectfully, without wasting anyone's time.

4. Be fluent in non-Bible-ese. People today are far removed from a biblical understanding. The average American may know more about the Star Wars universe than the New Testament worldview. Thus we must start with people where they are, not where we want them to be. Terms such as *gospel* and *sin* have deep meanings for you, but they likely have little meaning to those you're trying to reach. Darrell Bock of Dallas Theological Seminary, who is (among other things) executive director of Cultural Engagement there, told me that he encourages his students to exegete their cultures as they exegete the Scriptures. We need to clearly understand the interface between them and find our starting point for discussion. Do lots of listening when you talk to people in your community. Learn how they think, what they dream, what they fear.

5. Get comfortable with disequilibrium. The world is out of balance for the foreseeable future. The dial is not going to shift back to Christendom on the great clock of Western culture. We need to master our theological basics and then ride the waves of

change. Embrace the madness! Owning the faith essentials while engaging the community will create around you a culture of change and transformation. Express your joy in what God is doing so that the people around you celebrate rather than panic. Erwin McManus uses revolving staff assignments—no one should do one thing for more than three years, he says—to expose his leaders to various angles of ministry. He isn't *weathering* the turbulence; he's exploiting it!

NEXT STEPS

- Step outside your field of expertise and identify an entrepreneurial person in another field of education, the arts, business, advertising, marketing, or online enterprise and pay them for a day to let you job-shadow them. You may have to go out of the way, and it may cost you time and money. This is an investment in your future, a continuing education move for you. Look for their influencers. Who shaped them and how?
- Second, get with an unbeliever, not as a project, but as a friend, and get to know that person deeply. This will require authenticity. (Christians aren't always good with authenticity.) Let creativity flow out of relationships with unbelievers that helps move you toward apostolic genius.

PROFILE: ERWIN MCMANUS

He is elusive. At times he can be abstract. He is an artist. At the soul level, that's who he is: an authentic artist. Creative, a futurist, an innovator.

All these descriptors fit his setting: Hollywood. Erwin McManus is a pastor who was custom-made for the epicenter of creativity and imagination.

"Erwin is very hands-on to the course and direction of Mosaic," says Chad Becker, who has worked closely with McManus for fifteen years. "It is Erwin's ability to read and see the future that draws people like him to Mosaic." Using Tom Rath's popular book *Strengths Finder,* Chad classifies McManus as a futurist who peers over the horizon and lets the future pull him into tomorrow.[3]

"God steers us in the direction of his kingdom, his purpose, his passions," he says. "His desire is not to conform us, but to transform us. Not to make us compliant, but to make us creative. His intent is never to domesticate us, but to liberate us."[4]

McManus has always been impatient with the way creative people are eyed warily by the church as troublemakers and polluters of orthodoxy. Indeed he's seen as an iconoclast, someone who challenges the status quo at every turn. Mosaic saw two words that helped to explain its LA environment: *entertainment* and *change.* In terms of the latter, McManus has embraced change and sought to guide it. He speaks of Everett Rogers's chart on the innovators' scale of adaptability[5] (below) that shows the bell-curve process of change from the earliest innovators to the latest skeptics, who were dragged kicking and screaming into new conditions.

The leadership at Mosaic considers their church to be one of the few churches in the nation that was in the top 2 percent of innovative contributors to post-Christendom. *Relevant* magazine recently rated Mosaic as one of the most innovative churches in North America for unleashing the creativity of its members.[6] Most megachurches, McManus feels, are far more conservative about change, nestled at best in the "early majority of the change process." Laggards, of course, are those who push back and fight for the old, established ways.

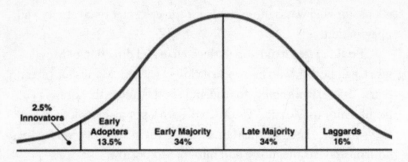

At Mosaic, nothing is taken for granted.

McManus was among the first to engage the implications of postmodern thinking for the church and to speak prophetically on how the church should respond. While he is a maverick in his thinking and leadership, he continues to raise up and push to the center of the stage the next generation of leaders. He can be elusive and hard to pin down. It's important to him to leave the church healthier and more fruitful than he found it. But now as well as later, he wants to lead movements.

McManus is committed to the classic historical gospel as it impacts the culture of this world within this moment. And he believes that to communicate that gospel to this particular world, change must occur for the messengers and creativity must become the order of the day.

$$\text{——— TEN ———}$$

FROM ADDITION TO MULTIPLICATION

Raising an Extended Family

MY SON CALEB IS THE FAMILY GENIUS. HE'S A WEST POINT GRADUATE, and when he's in town, he dazzles and astounds us. Sometimes more than we want to be dazzled and astounded. For example, there was the time he asked me the penny question.

Caleb walked into my office with a smile on his face. He stood at my desk, looked at me, and said, "What would you rather have? A million dollars today—or one penny today, doubled every day for a month?"

"Have you gotten a sketchy new job I need to know about?"

"Just answer the question, Dad."

I stared back as the wheels began to turn in my head. Those wheels squeak a lot. I haven't really oiled and maintained the math ones very well, I have to admit. Figuring out the tip at a restaurant is a high-intensity project for the wheels in my head.

Then again, did I really need to do the math? A million dollars is a tidy sum. It has a lot of zeroes in it; I do remember that. And a penny is as small as you can go. And thirty days? Well it was obvious to me that on the second day you'd get two cents. Third day you'd get four cents. Eight cents. Sixteen cents . . .

This one seemed like a no-brainer; in other words, the perfect question for me. "I'll take the million," I said.

"Good call, Dad. You just turned down five million, three hundred sixty-eight thousand, seven hundred nine dollars and twelve cents."

"No way."

"And if it's a thirty-one-day month—*ten* million plus, because it doubles *again*."

He got me. I stared at him for a moment before saying, "I bet you can't name the seven key transitions a Resurgent Church must make to thrive in a post-Christendom culture."

He chuckled and wandered away to the kitchen to plague his mother.

When he was out of sight, I pulled up a calculator app on my computer and started tapping away. I still thought he was full of beans. How could a penny, doubled only thirty times, end up at five million dollars?

Yet what he had really shown me was how grossly we underestimate the exponent. Addition impresses us, while multiplication just seems like a slightly better version of the same thing. At first, that's how it appears: sixty-four whole cents after a full *week* in Caleb's offer! Day fourteen is still a little under eighty-two bucks, and that's halfway through.

But during that third week, things start to get serious. At day twenty-one you're past ten thousand dollars. At day twenty-eight, you're past a million. Now we're talking about some *real* cash.

This is not a hard concept. Multiplication by itself spirals wildly. A grade-school kid can grasp that. But it's an *overlooked* concept.

What happens when we overlook it in the kingdom economy? We think of *adding* to the church family rather than multiplying ourselves. If we add a member a month to our church, we add twelve new members in a year. If we multiply ourselves—which happens when the new members themselves do the duplication—we become a social phenomenon. We transform the community and ultimately the world.

A more familiar concept that captures the same idea is the idea of going viral. Internet videos go viral. So do catchphrases and ideas and the Internet meme.

When we speak of that viral quality, of course, we're drawing from the biological idea of a virus, something capable of jumping from host to host to replicate itself. And that's a very crucial understanding, superior to the mathematical or financial analogies, because it captures the *contagious* quality of this growth. Growth takes on a life of its own.

Addition happens through grunt work: plodding, stubborn effort. Multiplication happens not through *multiplied* grunt work and plodding effort—that strategy would break down quickly—but through people coming into contact with something irresistible. No one is selling anything to them; their eyes are open and they're saying, "Where can I get that?"

We don't read about the disciples going door to door with tracts in Acts: "Hi, we're James and John, and we'd like to invite you to a meeting that's really unpopular with the Romans and religious leaders but based on our leader, whom they put on the cross, and requiring a whole lot of self-sacrifice and possibly death." Instead, we read:

> And day by day, attending the temple together and breaking bread in their homes, they received their food with glad and generous hearts, praising God and having favor with all the people. And the Lord added to their number day by day those who were being saved. (Acts 2:46–47)

Translation: They went viral. They added day by day, and soon they numbered in the thousands. What was contagious? The joy. The charisma of the Holy Spirit. The first-century Christians had something that others wanted, and within three centuries, the faith of a handful of disciples had outpaced the Roman Empire itself.

Twenty-first-century Christians need to rediscover viral faith.

WE LIVE THROUGH OUR CHILDREN

A discussion of exponential growth can sound like a world of fantasy to those struggling simply to keep the church doors open. As we saw in the opening chapter, the majority of churches in the United States have peaked in growth and find themselves somewhere on the downhill slope that only leads in one sad direction. The best research seems to suggest churches grow and decline just like people, or actually, even more rapidly—that is, their growth spurts come in the teenage years (first fifteen), and a slow decline may begin at about age thirty-five.[1] If we need to start thinking in terms of multiplication instead of addition, here's another paradigm shift we need: thinking in terms of new churches rather than desperately bolstering old ones.

As parents, we understand this. We invest in our kids. Sure, we continue to care for ourselves. In midlife, we try to eat right and work out. But we understand that our most important legacy will not be through the aging bodies we inhabit, but through those of the children we hatch and dispatch. Our children bring us fulfillment, and our grandchildren deliver hope, because we know we're touching the future through them.

The psalmist says that the children of our youth are like arrows in the hands of a warrior, so we might as well have a quiver full of them (127:4–5). I love the image of the archer firing those arrows into the sky, not knowing where they'll land. Children are our best way to touch tomorrow.

Churches are living organisms no less than we are. They have life cycles; there are things they'll never do as well as younger churches. So we need a quiver full of arrows. Our work is to fire them into the community, across the globe to make their mark. Our arrows, of course, are new churches.

Many church leaders need to realize that the struggle to keep the old church afloat may actually dwindle in importance compared to what that church owes to the future of Christianity—or even simply to our current communities. But an aging board of deacons or elders must be heard, and they love their own establishment; they don't get this planting thing. "Why can't we just do a better job of reaching people with our own church?" they ask.

We need to answer those voices with the words of church growth specialist C. Peter Wagner: "The single most effective evangelistic methodology under heaven is planting new churches."[2]

This we know by now. The most efficient and fruitful investment of our resources is to shift our focus from addition to multiplication. We need to stop thinking in terms of surviving and begin thinking of how we can thrive: through the work of new congregations strategically planted.

Someone came to Jesus and asked him why his disciples hadn't gotten the memo from the old-school religious leaders. Nothing about Jesus and his followers resembled the familiar ways of doing religion. Jesus replied:

> No one puts a piece of unshrunk cloth on an old garment, for
> the patch tears away from the garment, and a worse tear is made.
> Neither is new wine put into old wineskins. If it is, the skins

burst and the wine is spilled and the skins are destroyed. But new wine is put into fresh wineskins, and so both are preserved. (Matt. 9:16–17)

In other words, sometimes it's best to stop patching up that beloved old coat and put on a new and stylish one. And new wine needs a new container. We need to ask whether we've become too attached to the trappings of our faith rather than the new wine of the gospel, always as fresh and immediate as tomorrow's headlines. Starting new, contextual community churches is the way to do that.

When we think of traditionally evangelistic, traditionally church-starting congregations, a name that quickly surfaces is that of Southern Baptists. Yet between 2003 and 2005, that denomination netted zero growth in new churches. In a given year, it was discovered that only one Southern Baptist church in seven assisted actively in the planting of a new church.[3]

In my studies of Resurgent Churches, on the other hand, one of the more encouraging findings was that incarnational, missional churches have church planting very high on their priority lists. It's not that they occasionally cosponsor a friend in the next county wanting to open a church; they are proactive, strategic, and visionary about planting. They often bring on qualified full-time staff to oversee church planting. And the congregation knows all about it, because the victories of starting new churches are celebrated frequently.

We live during a tremendous surge of interest in church planting, as the message has finally come across to a significant number of church leaders. The incarnational, evangelistic task in a post-Christendom world is daunting, and our aging, last-century congregations simply aren't up to the task. There has been a surge in the number of books, conventions, and publicity about church planting. Some of our sharpest, most creative thinkers are devoting themselves to new and innovative launches.

It was only a generation ago that planting seemed to be something assigned to the B-team of ministry; the perception of some ministers was that they were being banished to the boondocks if they couldn't cut it in the big building. Now, that equation has reversed itself. Young ministers are highly interested in what they perceive to be the creative cutting edge of ministry.

Nor are the new assignments scattershot or makeshift. They tend to involve internships for the proposed planters, with onsite training and seminars with assessments, mentoring, equipping, shadowing, and commissioning. Thousands of aspiring planters attend the coastal Exponential conferences, which Ed Stetzer has wryly called "Six Flags over Church-Planting."[4]

The popular new formula is far more disciplined than it was in the past. Planters, with some degree of sacrifice, recruit a team to help do the work, then live in the proposed community for a year simply to get the heartbeat of the neighborhood and to build as many local relationships as possible. And deeply entwined in the DNA of the new church is the idea of reproduction on the other end. Within the first few years, this church will send out shoots and put down seeds for new churches. Otherwise we could never use the word *exponential.*

Churches are started in homes, schools, pubs, theaters, shopping centers, coffee shops, and even other churches with extra space. We must be flexible if we want to be contextual.

THE MULTISITE OPTION

One of the faces of the church planting movement has been the strategy of going multisite. The idea was that the mother church knew its mission and strategy best, so why not reproduce it as faithfully as possible by using technology? It fit the branding emphasis of contemporary marketing in the early part of this century. A popular teaching pastor would now be available in different parts of town—or even other towns—through closed-circuit television. In a typical setting, a different-style worship band and a more hip coffee bar might be available during services at a secondary site. The two locations would be unified by the same message transmitted by video and also by church government, philosophy, and funding.

According to figures offered by the Southern Baptist North American Mission Board, in 1990 there were fewer than ten multisite churches. In 2000 there were fewer than one hundred. By 2004 however, there were at least fifteen hundred.[5] By 2010 Leadership Network identified three thousand multisite churches with a 90 percent success rate,[6] and seven of the ten fastest-growing churches were using multiple sites.[7]

Not only was the multisite idea working, but it was demonstrably quicker, more efficient, and in some ways more sustainable. It was highly contextual because it fit so neatly into different neighborhoods and socioeconomic groups.

From the beginning, of course, there were questions. Was this uncomfortably close to fast-food franchising? Did it feed on the problem of so-called superstar-driven church marketing, so familiar in evangelicalism, so that traditional pastors would eventually be crowded out by a small handful of telegenic icons? And what was the long-term model for a site to become a living, breathing congregation with its own fully formed personality? Is there even a biblical model for multisite? Are multisites sterile? Can we point to third- and fourth-generations of church plants out of multisites?

MOVING BEYOND MULTISITE

Mosaic Church is a good example of the maturing process of the planting movement. Initially aggressive in its enthusiasm for multisite growth, Mosaic has shifted somewhat in its approach. Multisite was its preferred strategy for planting, but now there is again one Mosaic campus. All its various sites have been commissioned and set free as their own congregations.

Chad Becker, who carried the job of navigator for Mosaic, spoke of several criteria that were considered before these sites were commissioned from campuses to full-fledged churches.

1. Community. Each of the campuses had strong, healthy, and viable communities. There were generally between two hundred and four hundred active participants. Some of these campuses were under Mosaic's care during times of struggle. When they became healthier and could sustain themselves, they were commissioned.

2. Live Teaching. Each new congregation, of course, could provide its own teaching and preaching. If they'd been dependent upon Mosaic for messaging, they wouldn't have been ready.

3. Season in Life. Sometimes it's clear that it's time for your child to move out. This was the case with these campuses. They could care for themselves. They could train their own leaders. They were developing their own teachers and planting their own churches. Aging children at home, according to Becker, simply isn't the healthy and natural course of life.

Mosaic has raised some interesting questions about the future of multisite church plants. We know it's an idea with some benefits. It can be cost-efficient and leader-efficient. It's adaptable and proven. But is it truly the best option for producing healthy, sustainable, reproducible, fully contextual churches?

Church builders are familiar with an old saying: what you win them with is what you win them to. I could draw a huge crowd to my church if I managed to rope LeBron James to appear as a guest speaker. But I'd only have proven that I can win people to LeBron James. I want to win them to Jesus, and if people keep attending our church, it will have to be because they're interested in Jesus. There's nothing about me that's worth getting up on Sunday morning for.

Recently one of America's more influential pastors stepped down during a controversy. At the time his church had eleven multisite campuses who now had questions about their identities apart from the highly popular teaching of this pastor. The mother church shut down its multisite organization and released all eleven campuses. They changed their names and became independent congregations, making fresh starts. This is not to suggest that the church or its multisite organizations were built on one man's superstar status; certainly these campuses were bearing fruit and winning disciples on their own. The point is that the most obvious strength of that strategy—a name-brand teacher—can quickly turn from being a huge asset into its greatest vulnerability. This is one of the reasons the multisite approach is viewed with some ambivalence by some planters.

3SELF CHURCHES

The goal of church planting is to produce churches that are self-sustaining, self-propagating, and self-governing. This is known as the 3self measurement. This measurement isn't new century or post-Christendom; it's simply good missiology. Henry Venn, a nineteenth-century Church of England minister, is credited with being the first to urge this approach to missions.

These three criteria have been Mosaic's guides for launching their campus sites into full-fledged churches. Once a site has clearly fulfilled these indicators on the classic missiological grid, they're seen as ready for independence.

When we talk about churches remaining tethered to a mother

church in any of these three criteria, we describe that as multisite. Multisite strategy has been successful during the last fifteen years or so, and it can be seen as a creative idea that has borne good fruit. I believe the sites should be a means to an end rather than an end in themselves. We're not franchising and extending the church brand; we're spreading the name of Jesus. And looking to the future, we believe the ancient and traditional model of an indigenous church within a community is the wisest plan.

We do not need to take the shortcut of relying on specially anointed teachers who offer special crowd appeal. The Spirit dispenses gifts, including the gifts of teaching and preaching. He has always raised up believers for times and places of need. Our job as the mother church is to plant the seeds, equip the saints, and work alongside those saints until they're fit for ministry and ready to do some equipping themselves. As Paul says, "What you have heard from me in the presence of many witnesses entrust to faithful men who will be able to teach others also" (2 Tim. 2:2).

That's a rule of full—not partial—reproduction, and it's been the plan for twenty centuries. But by planting churches that develop their own leaders, we produce a bumper crop of teachers and other ministers for the next generation. We train and equip so that others can train and equip. It may be more demanding, difficult, and inefficient at first, but the long-term results will be healthier, fully operating, and ministering congregations for the body of Christ.

With all this said, the important point remains: smart churches start churches. As we've already seen, the most successful and fruitful congregations in America are busy about the work of reproducing themselves. In my study I never found the idea that it's simply our duty to do this or that would be a healthy project for us. Instead, planting was an initiative that was a natural reflex to dynamic, energetic congregations where the Spirit was moving. Living creatures don't need to be told to be fruitful and multiply; God hides it in their DNA.

Nor did I find the normal human tendency is to become self-involved over time and lose the missional drive. These are nearly all churches that are ramping up their plans, looking for ways to be even quicker about their planting, even more fruitful. When we find a neighborhood that needs a living, loving new church, and we fill that need, it's indescribably satisfying. We want to do it again. We want to do it twice as often, three times as often. We want viral growth of the kingdom of God. The fuel for church planting is always joy rather than rugged obedience, and it's the joy and passion that comes across to the people we want to reach in those communities. That's the Acts 2 dynamic.

On the other hand I've read about churches who are among the sick and dying of our national congregations. Some of them have realized their obsessing on survival and nursing their own wounds were more than half of the problem. They've begun to pour what resources they've had into the future and the kingdom by planting churches. And what would you expect to be the result? The mother churches saw an uptick in their own health. Planting is good for everybody.

We were born to reproduce, to give once we've received, to teach, to train, to commission. If we could only begin to understand the joy of being obedient to that design, we'd have fulfilled the Great Commission a long time ago.

NEXT STEPS

Answer the following questions:

1. How is your church currently involved in reproducing new churches?

2. If your church uses the multisite model, do you see this as an end or a means to an end? What does the second-generation multisite look like? (Your church's grandchild.) Does it look deformed after only one generation?

3. How can your church be a part of helping other churches revitalize or reinvent themselves into a new Resurgent, Incarnational Church?

4. Does your denomination or network affiliation have a church-planting division that you as a church can work alongside as you work with other churches to help them in planting?

From these and other questions, begin to formulate a plan to take two steps forward this next year and three the next toward being an exponential church.

PROFILE: PLANTING AT THE SUMMIT

Soon after J. D. Greear became pastor of Homestead Heights Baptist Church in Raleigh-Durham, the church underwent a revitalization process that included a new name: The Summit Church.

Greear realized the first act of the Holy Spirit after Pentecost was to start a church. He decided he could do a lot worse than to follow that lead.

The Summit Church, like many churches that have flourished in this century, has had great success with the multisite model. There are seven campus sites in the Raleigh-Durham area, and the church is looking toward starting more. A new campus is generally started in an area where a significant number of members live. From that group, a core is drawn to help birth a new campus. From inception, new campuses are tightly interwoven with the mother church.

Greear and his staff have a strong vision for the Raleigh-Durham area, and it's about saturating that area with the gospel by multiplying campuses and planting gospel-centered churches. The idea is to have a Summit campus within a fifteen-minute drive from everyone in the metropolitan area.

When considering the Summit Church's enduring commitment to the multisite approach, it's important to remember this church's highly specialized understanding of this specific community: young, high-tech, and academic. Approximately one quarter of the church's members are undergraduate or graduate students— a staggering figure probably unmatched anywhere. The Summit Church seeks to mobilize its fifteen hundred students for mission work and careers in places where new churches can be planted.

Yet the Summit Church has also planted twenty-three noncampus churches around the United States. Plants focus on strategic cities. Pastors are trained through a residency program and sent out with members sometimes recruited from the Summit Church. Unlike the campuses, these are independent and autonomous churches, though they're still considered part of a network, and every attempt is made to stay in touch for encouragement and advice.

The Summit Church is an example of a Resurgent Church that is growing more intense and visionary in its incarnational aspirations. When I first studied this congregation in 2009, the vision was ambitious but simple: start one thousand churches in this generation—a memorable goal with a good, round figure. Since then, the church has developed a network that includes a residence program for planters.

At the time of my first visit, 22 churches had been planted: 13 across the United States and 9 internationally. By 2014 there were 113 church plants: 23 in the United States and 90 internationally—58 in South Asia alone. Much of that, of course, occurred during the worst part of the Great Recession. If the law of exponential growth holds true, the numbers will continue to grow even more impressively, and that 1,000 in this generation will come to pass and be surpassed.

The Summit Church not only dreams big, it covers the details. It wants to plant churches locally and globally, but it's prepared to do the work of equipping that's necessary for that to occur.

For those who complete the residency program and qualify to plant churches, there is financial support over a three-year period, with startup assistance up to $100,000. On April 24, 2015, 153 members were commissioned to plant twenty-five US churches. Each church plant, in turn, is challenged to plant another church in three years and five churches in ten years.

It's an understatement to say we need more churches with the Summit Church's vision and entrepreneurial spirit.

---------------- ELEVEN ----------------

FROM DENOMINATIONS TO NETWORKS

The New Face of Cooperation

DENOMINATIONALISM BEGAN, AT LEAST IN THE WESTERN CHURCH, with Martin Luther. After all, Western European Christianity was almost exclusively Roman Catholic before the quiet but stubborn Wittenberg professor made his stand in the face of the pope's befuddled fury.

The idea of a denomination—a *variety* of Christianity—made no more sense than a variety of water. There was only one church in those nations. But in 1517, when Protestantism became a movement, things changed. After a while it became practical for followers of Luther to distinguish themselves from other Christians, and they began calling themselves Lutherans. But this didn't please the founder of their movement. Luther said,

> I ask that people make no reference to my name; let them call themselves Christians, not Lutherans. What is Luther? After all, the teaching is not mine. Neither was I crucified for anyone . . . . How then should I—poor, stinking maggot-fodder than I am— come to have people call the children of Christ by my wretched

157

name? Not so, my dear friends; let us abolish all party names and call ourselves Christian.[1]

It seems now like a well-intentioned but naive outlook. Inevitably schisms were going to happen. Wherever two or more are gathered, arguments ensue. Few things are more disorganized than organized religion.

As of 2014 the Center for the Study of Global Christianity at Gordon-Conwell Theological Seminary estimated there were 45,000 Christian denominations—and an increase of a staggering 10,000 *distinct denominations,* give or take, in the past decade. In 1900 the total was 1,600.[2] In post-industrial society, where people can think and question and argue doctrine with greater freedom, Christian groups have multiplied like rabbits. Then those rabbits have grown, matured, and become very set in their ways.

From a post-Christendom vantage point, never have denominations mattered less. This is true for Christians and seekers alike. They are largely relics of the institutionalization of the church.

Pastors have begun to find that the old reliable in-jokes ("I'll close the sermon a little early so we can beat the Methodists to the cafeteria") likely draw blank stares. People don't know the doctrinal fine points, and for the most part they don't really care. In past centuries people died for the stands they took on, for example, believers' baptism. For people today, we might as well argue about how many angels can dance on the head of a microchip.

Denominations have been much more than doctrinal coalitions. They've been large-scale cooperatives for getting things done, particularly missions. They've provided levels of authority, in some cases, to maintain discipline or oversee the church's identity and work in a larger region. They've provided study materials, seminaries, and any number of needful things that a small church could never have accessed otherwise. So we can't be too eager to throw out the baby with the bathwater. Denominations have been used of God, and they surely will continue to be—in one form or another—in the days ahead.

But just as individual churches and leaders must learn to understand the new realities of our culture, so must denominations and also parachurch ministries.

Our major Protestant denominations were built for bygone eras, and they served those eras well. But they're showing signs of age. The major denominational groups and parachurch groups can no longer take for granted any of their systems or strategies or institutions. Everything needs to be rethought, because the world is no longer the old and familiar one, and denominational identities are puzzling and even off-putting to many of the people we're trying to reach.

This has been self-evident for a good while. Churches have been far less likely to embed their denominational identities in their names. Saddleback Community Church was planted in Orange County, California, as early as 1980 as a Southern Baptist church that didn't advertise its affiliation. It's rare for a new Baptist church plant to identify its roots in its name. Some legacy Baptist churches are even taking Baptist out of their names (the Summit Church and Mosaic being examples).

Ed Stetzer, executive director of LifeWay research, said, "I've started multiple churches, none of which had a denomination in the name. It wasn't even a conversation. It was just an assumption that we're trying to reach unchurched people so we don't want to have additional barriers."[3]

The Southern Baptist Convention itself debated a name change not long ago, acknowledging that, particularly in the Northeast, the brand wasn't seen as a plus to potential attenders. It was hard to ignore research that suggested denominational churches were four times more likely to be perceived as formal and three times more likely to be perceived as old-fashioned as well as structured and rigid.[4]

In fairness we find that people aren't exactly *closed* to denominational churches; if they can see their needs will be met, and if the church seems to be *about* spiritual life rather than a church's obscure doctrinal distinctions, they won't be put off. But as a whole, denominational churches are flat in growth while nondenominational evangelical churches show a dramatic increase in numbers by comparison.

It's too early to proclaim the death of denominations. There are things churches can do together cooperatively that simply can't be done alone or even in very small groups. On the other hand, we have to realize times are changing, and the way those denominations approach the world—and the way churches approach the denominations—will have to change as surely as everything else in this post-Christendom world. The plain truth is that many of these cooperative tasks are being done better by smaller, more focused networks.

OWN THE MISSION

Church denominations grew with Protestantism and were specially galvanized by the American idea of separation of church and state. The various denominations allowed churches to distinguish their set of beliefs and express them. It was a new and specific form of self-government that came in with distancing the church from secular government. But the great idea was not that of control but *cooperation*. There is strength in numbers, and churches banded together to do what no one church could do alone.

Resurgent, Incarnational Church leaders, however, have rethought that equation. The old idea transmitted to church members—"Just write a check to the denomination, and they'll send out missionaries"—

is unappealing to postmodern minds. People want a sense of involvement in their global ministry. Not only do they want to know where their money is going, but they want to participate in the adventure as much as possible. Short-term mission trips weren't practical in the era when mission boards were organizing. Missionaries were formally trained, lifetime-committed individuals or families who appeared occasionally to offer slideshows of their work to yawning congregations. A missionary was a specialist rather than a designation for all Christians to share.

My own studies show that Resurgent Churches are missionally driven, globally engaged, and hands-on in their approach to sending missionaries, as well as other matters once dominated by parent denominations. J. D. Greear of the Summit Church commented that denominations should be seen as tools to use, when necessary, for doing the work of ministry, but not as proxies or substitutes to cover areas of mission and thus free the church to focus on preaching and programs. The Summit Church partners with the Southern Baptist Convention, but Greear and his staff feel that the denomination, if it wants more cooperation, should commit itself to modernizing and trimming its cumbersome bureaucracy.

Mosaic in Los Angeles has an even more ambivalent relationship to its Baptist roots. The church considers itself, for practical purposes, nondenominational. Many members would be puzzled to learn they've been attending a Baptist church, because it's not a subject that comes up. Even so the church partners significantly with the International Missions Board of the SBC, sending out fifty of its eighty family units to mission assignments.

I do not detect any bias against denominations as such. It's just that the churches take their ministry so seriously that they're insistent on owning it. If a denomination can help them with their work, that's a positive. If they can get it done quickly, more efficiently, and especially through their own people and resources—including other networks—that will be the better choice. Resurgent Churches aren't reactionary to the denominations' whims and programs, but they are aggressively active toward leading movements. The new way invites all of like mind to join them, denominations included, if they don't mind the church leading the charge.

People tend to define themselves by their work. The man sitting next to you on the airplane will give you his name first and his occupation second. Job is the primary sense of identity in the modern world. Resurgent Churches think of themselves in the same terms. They define themselves by their mission, their clear sense of purpose.

This wasn't always necessarily true. A church member would immediately describe himself as a Methodist, a Presbyterian, a Baptist, or some other affiliation. Churches today, along with their members, understand themselves by mission rather than identification. They will first tell you what their church envisions doing rather than how they align themselves with a broad ecclesiastical classification.

Denominations have been built on a foundation of doctrinal agreement. Denominations have typically come into the world through painful birthing processes—usually some struggle over basic beliefs. (To this day, denominations are breaking up into newer ones based on doctrinal squabbling—one of the factors most likely to drive people away from them.) Once the points of doctrine are all in order under this model, mission can be pursued. This will mean that identity is built on the details of belief and also that denominations with clashing doctrines will have trouble cooperating in the mission field.

There's been a paradigm shift with Resurgent Churches in the post-Christendom world. Mission actually trumps doctrine. This in no way suggests that doctrine is shaky or secondary to Resurgent Churches; it's always present as a foundation of ultimate identity, and it guides message and mission. But these churches are energized by the mission they're pursuing. They'll gladly work with people of varying views on non-first-tier doctrines. For the urgency of the mission, second- and third-tier doctrinal disagreements can simply be ignored.[5]

What is that mission? It can—and should—mean something different to every church. It's another advantage of churches owning their mission rather than subcontracting it to a denominational agency. One church may rally together with another congregation across town to address a glaring local social problem. Another church may bond with a need somewhere across the globe, in a place meaningful to both congregations for one reason or another. A church can have a passion for translating the Scriptures or sharing the *Jesus* film or simply planting new churches in New England, where Christianity is fading. A church can be dedicated to reaching Millennials and feel the need to share a close friendship with another church with that same passion.

When churches lead with mission rather than doctrinal devotion, there is less argument, less bureaucracy, and fewer barriers.

BODY OF WORK VERSUS BODY OF BELIEF

Denominations are beginning to get the message. For one thing, they see the model of Resurgent, Incarnational Churches. For another, they feel less secure in a post-Christendom world where there is less of a luxury to be picky about the finer points of doctrine. Some denominations are beginning to cooperate with one another, even when they can't agree on certain belief points. Any Christian leader who doesn't feel a sense of urgency in these times is out of touch. Therefore there is a movement toward leading with mission.

Eddie Gibbs observed that denominational executives are most in need of that wakeup call. They're not on the front lines of battle, and they're invested in addressing institutional and bureaucratic issues. They're wrestling with tight budgets and downsizing. But it's the denominational workers on the ground, he said—working at the edge of mission—who are most aware of these changes and most likely to be starting to address them.[6]

Mission versus doctrine is not an either/or dichotomy. There's no reason we can't have sound doctrine and soaring mission. But the reality is that postmodern people don't engage with historical doctrinal truth in the same way as people did in the past. They're most likely to respond to genuine and visible ministry.

Resurgent Churches have learned a powerful truth. It pays to define ourselves by what we're *for* rather than what we're *against*. What postmodern Christians want to know is, "What are we going to do in this world? How shall we then live?" Resurgent Churches are saying, "This is who we are. Look at our body of work, and at the proper time, we'll discuss our body of doctrine with you."

People respond to action-based churches. Once again, it hardly needs to be said that there's no implication that preaching, doctrine, and the rest don't matter. But churches and denominations alike, if they want to be resurgent, must lead with mission and with purpose; they must rally around what needs to be done rather than convene committees on what needs to be condemned.

Here is how this truth has impacted my personal church leadership. Grace Point Church arose from Southern Baptist roots—in particular, my background and mission work as a Baptist. But as we planted this church, we chose to voluntarily affiliate with Southern Baptists. It's a subtle distinction that established that something other than denominational authority was driving the birth and raising of our congregation. It guaranteed our autonomy. (It should also, perhaps, be mentioned that Southern Baptists are historically a *congregational* denomination; that is, what Grace Point did is fairly normative. The SBC is a *cooperative* enterprise rather than a controlling one.)

Grace Point is not a Southern Baptist church per se, but it is one that chooses to cooperate and partner with the convention during this season of its life, particularly in key mission areas. We have a great relationship with Southern Baptists, and our theology is compatible too—but we own our mission and our purpose, and these, *rather than affiliation*, define our identity. Along with Baptist agencies, we affiliate with various non-Baptist global and local mission organizations. We lead with our purpose and choose our friends accordingly.

This creates a difference, of course. If you build your foundation on denomination, then you'll find yourself conforming to policies and procedures within your tribe. If you choose autonomy, there will be times when you're considered a rogue church or leader, and some will distrust you. Fruitfulness in mission renders all of that moot, however. What really matters is not being a good Baptist/Methodist/Presbyterian/Whatever, but being a rescue mission for the kingdom with a sense of urgency.

Those who are digging those new-church foundations need to do the extra work and take a good look around at the riches of contemporary network resources. We've seen the rise of groups such as Acts 29, Fresh Expressions, New Thing, Gospel Coalition, etc. These are helpful collectives, lean and agile at their specialties, for their specific "tribes" where Incarnational Churches can go to find support, counsel, and community. Many of these new networks have risen up in reflection of the new realities of church planting and missions as a whole, and they're built to be sleek and efficient in ways that denominations can't duplicate. An appendix at the end of this book lists a few of these networks.

Bob Roberts Jr. is the lead pastor at Northwood Church in the Dallas–Fort Worth metro area—one of the churches that was part of my study. I've found his insight helpful, this quote being an example:

I've discovered that all pastors, especially pastors of larger churches, are involved in something beyond their local church that gives impact to their local church. At the same time, they export elements from their local church to bless other churches and communities. Twenty years ago, that meant serving on boards with institutions and the denominations. Today, young people in the ministry want to invest time in areas where they can see results that go beyond religions bureaucracies.[7]

NETWORKS AND MOVEMENTS

Resurgent Churches are far more likely to be network-friendly rather than denomination-limited. Networks are nimble. They're more tightly focused, more dynamic, and custom-tailored to place and time. Networks, therefore, are movement catalysts. Resurgent Churches should begin with their calling, their mission, and define what God wants them to do. Then they should consider ways to network with as many causes, missions, *and* denominations as might be profitable in accomplishing that mission.

Networks may have a powerful life but a shorter life span than a denomination that is less nimble but built for duration. This is okay. Needs rise and dissipate, and with them our specialized responses. Tighter focus allows us to do this.

There are four qualities of networks that lead to dynamic movements.

1. **Organic affinities.** In our culture, people build smaller communities by seeking out other people with similar interests and forming affinity groups, or what Seth Godin calls *tribes*. (See chapter 6.) We call these tribes or groups organic because of the natural (unforced) way they form; birds of a feather flocking together. Certainly there are

theological affinity groups. For example, those who identify with the Gospel Coalition are bound by a common reformed theology. A nonexhaustive list of tribes can be found in the appendix of this book.

2. **Collective passion.** Will Mancini has referred to this idea as *apostolic esprit.* The defining question is, "What particular need or concern is the one that most energizes our group?" The answer can be a range of things, local or global. What is it about the world that most bothers us? What do we feel the strongest drive toward getting done?

For the Summit Church, the answer is clear and powerful: a passion for multiplication. The Summit Network is a movement that has come together to help plant churches nationally, and the churches they plant will share that affinity for reproducing themselves. It's impossible to talk to the lead pastor, his staff, or even active members without picking up on this powerful drive to create new churches. It's the Summit Church's collective passion.

There are movements that touch on the arts, on care for various diseases or conditions, on reaching teenagers or twenty-somethings, on reformation of worship or preaching or some other element of Christian experience, or simply on renewal and revival. In Christian history world mission, the translation of the Bible, the outlawing of slavery, and many other developments have risen from earlier versions of affinity groups and collective passion. Once these two elements come together, a spark is ignited and a movement can begin.

3. **Innovation catalyst.** Networks cause iron to temper iron, and the result is energy, creativity, and innovation. Everyone is possessed with a heartfelt desire to get something done, and suddenly there is a breakthrough. Someone thinks of a new

way to do things. Networks can become God's think tanks where ideas bounce off one another and new outlooks are first glimpsed.

Mancini, on the other hand, saw denominations as "think holes"—places where good ideas go to die. Bureaucracy suffocates creativity and passion.[8]

4. Mutual collaboration. Command and control is out in the Resurgent Church. Egos are checked at the door, and partners respect one another. When passion for mission is the main thing, pettiness dissolves. There is an eagerness for new ideas and direction as well as an "all hands on deck" spirit for pooling resources to get the work accomplished.

In Resurgent Churches and networks, top-down command is out. What we do find is a decentralized structure in which much of the creativity flows upward. And no one is threatened. No one worries about who gets the credit. People are freed up to be creative, and they're more willing to share their ideas when they know others will listen.

Leadership Network (LN), based in Dallas and founded more than thirty years ago by Bob Buford, is an example of an attempt to bring churches together around various affinities—multisite movements, city and global impact, leadership styles, and so on. LN invests time and effort in interviewing and selecting churches that share common passions. They place the leaders together for extended periods for the kind of cross-pollination discussed above. It's not uncommon for one leader to produce a solution for another's problem.

LN publishes helpful materials and spreads the news about what is and isn't working. At all times there's a spirit of mutuality that cannot be found in denominational settings. People are joined by their passions and their goals rather than their denominational roots.

In the tribal culture of our day, Seth Godin observed, there are "movement[s] waiting to happen, a group of people waiting to be energized."[9] Our God has always worked by creating mission hearts. We should be checking our passions as if they were e-mail from heaven. The Lord is telling us what he has in mind for us. And if he fills us with a sense of need, then he also gives us the power and opportunity to address those needs. Part of that is this modern ease of networking.

What about your passion? Your church? Who will come alongside you to help you get your mission done? The central wonder of our age is the ease of communication across vast distances. The wise will dedicate that power to the work of God's kingdom.

NEXT STEPS

Think it through: what are the top three values of your church?

Once you've decided on some firm answers, take that same question to your staff, lay leadership, new members, and guests who have just started affiliating with you. Make sure there is alignment in at least one core value.

Now consider a sister church within your denomination, network, or beyond that is farther down the road in development of that particular value.

1. Contact the leaders of that church and walk with them for a time. Allow them to mentor you as you become their protégé.
2. Seek out networks or associations you can join that are doing your central core value.

3. Fine-tune your core value in at least three ways over the next twelve months.

Then repeat! Make this an ongoing discipline of leading your church.

PROFILE: SUMMIT NETWORK

It's a bit startling to discover that the name of the director of Summit Network is Mike McDaniel. Before I go further, let's be clear—he and I are two different guys, though we share a common passion for church planting. Perhaps we need a network of same-named, same-vision church leaders!

Summit Network is the response to Pastor J. D. Greear's (and his church's) vision of planting one thousand churches in this generation. Greear was impressed early on that the Great Commission is a church-planting commission. In other words, it's God's way of spreading the gospel to every corner of the world.

This network is all about training, equipping, and sending those leaders. It's one thing to talk about one thousand new churches; it's another to come up with capable and like-minded leaders. Greear says the difference is in refusing to see churches as clusters gathered around a leader, but instead to see them as leadership factories that intentionally produce those leaders. "Pushing out leaders creates more leaders," he says.[10]

Summit Network emphasizes three distinctives:

- Gospel: Like so many Resurgent Churches and movements, the Summit Church places the word *gospel* at its epicenter. Everything proceeds from and to the character and message of Jesus, who is God incarnate in the world.

- Balance: The Summit Church avoids the eternal collision of either/or. The greatest truths are often found in tension. Can doctrine and mission exist in harmony? Evangelism and social ministry? Missional and attractional ministry? More often than we realize, the truth is found in a dynamic balance between two opposing extremes. The Summit Church attempts to create balanced, intelligent congregations.

- Multiplication: The fuel and passion of the Summit Network is the simple idea of reproduction by multiplication. Jesus may have focused on a few, but he preached to many, and he left a mandate to reach everyone. The Summit Network feels and creates an urgency to keep moving, keep being fruitful, keep adding to the number of new churches who love and follow Jesus. This means, of course, a constant focus on training and equipping; a constant calling out of new seed planters; and a constant awareness of the state of the mission field in every place where the gospel is to be brought.

The Summit Network is strategic about all that it does, so it targets key US cities and elsewhere and has already planted growing churches in Atlanta, Los Angeles, New York, Baltimore, Indianapolis, and Denver, as well as other places.

It's notable that this resurgent network partners with other networks: Acts 29, North American Mission Board, International Missions Board, and North Carolina Baptists.

——————— TWELVE ———————

FROM CUL-DE-SAC
TO GLOBAL

Increasing Your Church's Horizons

WHAT'S YOUR CHILD'S GLOBAL IQ?

If he or she is a typical product of American schools, then the score is probably too low.

The National Geographic–Roper Public Affairs 2006 Geographic Literacy Study took an advanced look at our children's grasp of world geography. What they found was that young adults between the ages of eighteen and twenty-four don't know too much about the world beyond these shores.

- Fewer than three in ten graduates felt it was important to know the locations of countries in the news.
- Two respondents in three could not find Iraq or Saudi Arabia on a map.
- Three in four couldn't find Iran or Israel.
- Seven out of eight couldn't find Afghanistan on a map of Asia.
- Three in ten thought the most heavily fortified border was between the United States and Mexico (instead of between North and South Korea).

173

The final report concluded that our young people are far from adequately prepared for an increasingly global future.[1]

You may think you know where I'm going with this—and you'd be wrong. I'm not heading into a harangue about losing our mission hearts in a self-obsessed world. My point is that, all this while, no matter what that study says, God is doing something special.

Gordon-Conwell Seminary's Center for the Study of Global Christianity published a study recently that concluded:

> The twenty-first century has witnessed the sending of international missionaries to all of the world's countries from almost every country. In 2010, Christians from all traditions sent out approximately 400,000 international missionaries; this figure does not include missionaries who were at work in their home countries.[2]

These figures also show the United States to be the top missionary-sending nation, with 127,000 missionaries sent (Brazil is second). During the twentieth century, during the slow fade of Christendom, more and more missionaries were actually sent out. Not that we should relax over any of these figures. The fields are still "white for harvest," as Jesus said two thousand years ago. The needs are great.

But even as postmodern thinking challenges the notion of evangelism, suggesting that one faith is more or less as good as another, even as post-Christendom whittles away at the old assumptions that we have a burden and responsibility to take our faith to the world, even as the hedonism and self-absorption of these entertainment-driven times render our culture into a nation of consumers rather than one of servanthood, even with all this, God is raising up Resurgent Churches with urgent passions for reaching the world.

We forget this simple fact: if you and I love God, it is because he first loved us. If we have a desire to be part of a Resurgent Church in the resurgent kingdom of God, it's because his Spirit is fueling that desire. And if we find people in our churches who suddenly burn to go across the globe and help plant churches, that's not because we've been good salespeople. It's not because we just have some really fine folks in our church. It's because God is kindling the fire. God is love, and love is mission.

He created this world and all its people. He yearns every day, more than any other thing, for those people to come home to his love and grace and restoration. This is why a Resurgent Church is a global church.

A NEW GLOBAL PASSION

In the previous chapter we discussed an age of movements. Networks can facilitate movements because they're built to respond quickly and creatively to that spark of the Holy Spirit, igniting men and women toward some godly goal.

Between 2010 and the present, according to the figures of the Center for the Study of Global Christianity, there has been a slight decrease in career missionaries but a great upsurge of short-term mission trips and projects. This is representative of what we're seeing in Resurgent Churches, as well as the fading of the familiar missionary paradigms. In the old, conventional system, aspiring missionaries reported to their denominational agencies, received their training, and boarded a boat to quietly pursue the Great Commission for us by proxy. The church members' job was to "pray, pay, and get out of the way." Perhaps at Christmastime we would write an extra little check for the foreign mission plan, but mostly it was another item in the church budget, left to the leadership to allocate.

The subject of missions was second, perhaps, only to tithing as the least desired preaching topic. And not infrequently was heard the question, "Why should we worry about ministry in some country across the ocean somewhere when we have things in our own neighborhood we should be attending to?" The leaders would stammer that Jesus said so, that's why.

This may still be the case in a great many churches; these words may cause a pain of familiarity for many readers. But I'm here to tell you, based on my study of Resurgent Churches, that a new profile of global mission, at the local church level, is rising.

It's almost counterintuitive actually. My study primarily concerned how churches were reaching their communities and how they were engaging increasingly postmodern attitudes. I found, of course, they've found new and creative ways to interact with their communities; they've approached American cities with an incarnational, "from the margins" attitude. Yet just as you'd expect their focus to be local, it has been . . . *glocal*.

We touched on glocalization in chapter 4. It's basically a holistic understanding of all that we're doing as missional people of God. We're not either/or servants but both/and servants because that's who God is. That's who God loves: the community and the world. The Great Commission is all-inclusive. It's explicitly glocal, mentioning both Jerusalem *and* "the end of the earth" (Acts 1:8). This doesn't leave us a box to check, selecting one or the other; it calls on us to be reaching around the corner and around the world simultaneously.

Resurgent Church leaders get that, and even as their hearts for their communities grow more passionate, they find themselves reaching past city limits, past national borders, and into other points on the globe. And they're doing that intelligently, asking, "Where can we be most strategic?"

Too many conventional missions are in places already saturated (if not perfectly) by the gospel. The new missionaries are asking, "Where are the unreached people? Where is the name of Jesus still unknown?"

Most encouragingly of all, even as our children may not be too good with maps, the young people in our church are catching up quickly. They're responding to the passion of their leaders for world missions. They're stepping forward to say, with the prophets, "Here I am. Send me." They're leaving for short-term mission trips of a few months or a year, and then returning to say, "I can no longer look upon this work as short term. This is something worth giving my life to. Sign me up for that, and forward my mail."

GIVE UP YOUR SMALL AMBITIONS

Christianity has become a self-directed thing in recent decades. People shop around for the church that will feed them and provide programs they can use as consumers. Our preaching followed the same direction, focusing on the popular felt-need agenda. How can I be a better husband? A better mother? How can I settle conflicts at work? How should I deal with depression? Loneliness?

We've tended to follow the cultural direction of a self-obsessed world, and it's not surprising that our churches show no life or vitality at a certain point. We've gotten away from the heat of the gospel.

Yet Resurgent Churches, as we've seen, are outward directed. These churches aren't self-obsessed but about being a part of something bigger than themselves. The personal needs of believers aren't neglected, but it's recognized that we can't grow without a powerful focus on mission and service.

Maybe one of greatest spiritual formation strategies isn't getting people into the church to pray, but rather getting people into the world praying. As a matter of fact, the best way to grow as a prayer warrior is to do missions, a challenge that forces us to our knees. The best way to grow in the Word is to take the Word to our communities, where we're forced to dig deeper into what God has told us. The irony is that the more we focus on self, the less we grow in godly selfhood. As Francis of Assisi put it, it's in giving that we receive.

The new wave of missions-sending doesn't wait for believers to become expert Christians; it calls them out, saying, "Come learn on the job. All along the way we'll get to know God by depending on him at the front lines. We'll learn the lessons of discipleship through the tasks that discipleship demands. When a fire is scorching the house, you don't enlist in a course in fire-fighting—you grab a hose, even if you make a mistake or two. The need is urgent. So let's give up our small ambitions and get to work." David Platt, president of the International Mission Board (IMB) the largest evangelical mission-sending agency, has called for believers to leverage their job, education, and retirement as the new mission paradigm of their organization.[3] Professional missionaries are being replaced by incarnational believers who are funded, fueled, and accountable to their Resurgent Churches and who will work beside one of the great sending agencies, such as IMB.

At Grace Point we've found that nothing builds fully formed disciples more effectively than mobilizing them for missions among the nations. For example, we've commissioned two hundred members to travel to a West African country for terms between two weeks and up to two years in a strategic long-term partnership. Our members are commissioned by Grace Point Church to be involved in all matters of spiritual and community development there. We talk a whole lot about giving our vacation time to God as the best decision any home could possibly make—the ultimate adventure. And we find that invitation resonates. We go into schools and teach. We work in the fields. We lend a hand in health clinics. We share food from a common bowl and live out of mud huts. We do life with them. During all these pursuits, we're representing Jesus, speaking the gospel at every opportunity, and looking toward planting churches.

The task of the day may be to lay bricks and build a house. But we're not fooled; we know we're really building people—some from Africa and some from Arkansas. This is a beautiful thing. In many villages in that area you'll find the dusty footprint that says Jesus has been there through his ambassadors from half a world away.

Our focus in this West African country has persevered through political coups d'état, terrorist threats, and Ebola. We talk about the BHAGs (big, hairy, audacious goals) of our church, and one of them is to see a target people move from unreached to reached within ten years.* We use the word *audacious* for a reason. That target is made of hundreds of thousands of people. We don't see ourselves as the agents for every soul's conversion, but together we can be the catalyst of a movement in our chosen corner of the vast continent.

You might ask, "That's great for the people over there. What's in it for the people over here?" It's a legitimate question. To see the answer, you'd have to spend a week with some of our people. (Or at least read the profile at the end of this chapter.) You'd have to feel the fire of passion in the hearts of our folks for West Africa. (Believe me, you'd feel it pretty quickly.)

Then you'd have to see all the lives of acquaintances back in the States who are touched by seeing it too. Living on mission transforms people like nothing else; God becomes bigger as the world grows smaller. It forces us to let God do what he's always wanted to do in us and through us.

Back home, at Grace Point, we see that our mission is in front of our eyes at every moment. If you want to meet with any committee we have, you'll do so in a room that bears boldly painted letters on the wall:

---

* Missiologists generally consider that a people group is reached when 2 percent or more of the population are evangelical followers of Christ.

Every congregation is a world missions strategy center.

—Henry Blackaby[4]

Even around town we're on world mission. Our church realizes it touches the world simply through its community of members. Our large corporate businesses draw in and send out people internationally. We've seen families join our church from China, their previous church being part of the underground Christian network in that nation. It makes an impression on our members, to say the least. More typically, as our businesses have sent their people (our members) to China, India, or some other location across the globe, there have been opportunities to serve Christ in their new communities. We've done training and commissioning while the employers have provided funding and windows of opportunity.

With or without the church—whether you're in northwest Arkansas or New York City or some other place—globalization is happening. As our kids would say, "It's a thing." In many cases, it's the world coming to us, up to and including other countries sending missionaries to our country. Whenever a new thing happens on the world scene, you can bet God has a new thing of his own to do, whether we're talking about technology, globalization, or even the tragic news of disasters. God is always on the move, always a heavenly step ahead of whatever we do, conceive, or experience. As far as the global village is concerned, we're receiving opportunities commensurate to the challenges. And we're seeing hearts and souls moved to answer the call.

At the same time, this new generation, known as Millennials, is often criticized, often microanalyzed, often bemoaned as lazy or self-absorbed or overly cynical. What we're finding is that for a generation supposedly answering to that description, there are remarkable numbers of young people stepping forward to insist on defining faith as godly service, wanting to go somewhere, make some sacrifice, and impact the world for Christ.

These kids are very different from their parents. They've grown up with less comfort and luxury than their parents, often more difficult family situations, and a more troubling and frightening world in general, in which global terrorism and world recession have been the norm. While some of these younger people are indeed cynical and even nihilistic, many others have moved in the opposite direction. They want to light a candle rather than curse the darkness.

They look around and see the hatred and bitterness toward those different from us in other countries, and love seems like a radical alternative. They look around and see despondency over financial struggle, and spiritual faith seems like a better way. From the ashes of our millennial chaos, God is doing a new thing. Would you expect anything different?

> The old distinction between home missions and foreign missions is made completely obsolete by today's global cities.
>
> —FRITZ KLING[5]

RESURGENT MISSION

The churches in my study were congregations that have been noted for their success. Observers have mostly studied how these churches relate to their communities, and of course there are many brilliant lessons to be learned in that regard. But what is most often missed is the global passion of Resurgent Churches. Again, this defies expectation in a culture so often self-obsessed and, at best, ambivalent toward the rest of the world. It challenges postmodern assumptions about diversity being the great goal and missions and evangelism being arrogant.

Where is there a more diverse culture than Los Angeles? And yet Mosaic was, at one time, sending one adult every month into full-time career-based mission. They kept that streak going for four years. The church has at least sixteen families overseas with long-term commitments to live and work missionally.

Pastor Erwin McManus observed,

From our community in Los Angeles we have social workers in New Delhi; artists in Istanbul; an aspiring chef in Paris; a dancer, a film editor, a soon-to-be doctor, and a fashion designer in New York; businesspeople in China; a psychologist and educator in Lithuania; an environmental engineer in Morocco; and the list goes on and on and on. I cannot overemphasize how difficult these people are to replace. Yet as much complexity as this brings and as much instability as this creates, it pales in comparison to watching lives being wasted on careers and occupations that were taken on as a result of obligation or lack of courage to pursue the dreams that were waiting to be realized.[6]

In other words he pointed out that Mosaic people are giving up their small ambitions.

The church, as founded by Jesus Christ, was a church on mission. Somewhere along the way, it became a church that (at best) *supported* missions. At all costs, we need to reverse that policy and get back to our roots as a global rescue operation rather than a local civic organization that focuses on comfort.

At the Summit Church in Raleigh-Durham, staff members will tell you that the word *missional*—so much in vogue across Christianity

—actually isn't used very often. When something is at the heart of who you are, it goes without saying. People don't require reminding when it's all over today's to-do list. J. D. Greear sees church as training for heavenly battle, for building one another up in order to do the work in the community and the world.

Greear makes a startling observation from Acts, his basic text for building and guiding the Summit Church. Out of forty miracles performed in this book, thirty-nine are accomplished *outside the church*. We sit in our Sunday school classes and ask one another why miracles don't happen anymore. Perhaps we wouldn't be wondering so much if we got outside the facilities and put our shoulder to the work appointed for us. Miracles occur at the intersection of light and darkness, of faith and challenge, of the church and the world. What exactly do we expect God to be doing through us as we huddle around a coffee pot, listen to a sermon, and then go back home? Can we let our churches settle for that kind of life?

The Summit Church believes in wise partnerships for accomplishing missions—in particular the North American Mission Board for planting efforts. Internationally, the Summit Church has worked closely with the International Missions Board as an overseas facilitator. Most of the individuals and families sent from the Summit Church have some level of affiliation with the IMB. They could be fully supported IMB missionaries, self-supporting but administered by IMB leadership, or they might be working in the international marketplace as partners with the IMB.

The Summit Church sends but it also gives. Mission giving has continued to increase as a part of the church's budget. Not all of this is earmarked for Baptist agencies. The church has increased its financial commitment to outside denominational mission from 2.6 percent to 6.7 percent in recent times.

NEXT STEPS

What can you do to begin to position your church for global mission?

- Open your mind. And your heart. The heart of a church cannot change until the hearts of its leaders are transformed. Ask God to show you other people, including those in nations we've opposed, the way he sees them. Think fairly and rationally: not every Muslim is a jihadist. Begin to pay greater attention to news and information about other parts of the world. Model the mind of Jesus: "When he saw the crowds, he had compassion for them, because they were harassed and helpless, like sheep without a shepherd" (Matt. 9:36).
- Open your home. Find out about hosting international guests for cultural learning experiences. More than 70 percent of international students will visit our universities and colleges for four years or more without ever setting foot inside an American home.[7] Be a good steward of the empty place setting and seat at the table—invite someone from the outside in. Given nothing more than a dinner table, God can do a new thing. Model New Testament hospitality: "Do not neglect to show hospitality to strangers" (Heb. 13:2).
- Open your calendar. Make time for a short-term international engagement. (If you want to open your mind and heart, this is the best possible way of making that happen.) Take your spouse and older children and spend a "mission-cation" among one of the least-reached peoples. Simply live with them and interact with them and watch God open doors. Model the vision of Paul: "At the same time, pray also for us, that God may open to us a door for the word, to declare the mystery of Christ, on account of which I am in prison" (Col. 4:3).

- Open your wallet. Our personal budgets need to be
transformed by the mind of Christ, and then our church
budgets can do likewise. The West has the most affluence
and access to the gospel. This affluence carries with it
a kingdom responsibility. Our priorities are seen in our
investments (Luke 12:34). Give generously but never
blindly. While many open their wallets first, I urge them to
do that second. Start instead by building relationships with
those whom you'd support. Allow yourself to have your
heart changed through personal involvement in missions,
and then giving won't even require discipline—it will
overflow from a compassionate heart. Model the generosity
of the gospel: "And he answered them, 'Whoever has two
tunics is to share with him who has none, and whoever has
food is to do likewise'" (Luke 3:11).

God has no small plans. He isn't content to stop with your life
or the life of your church. In the end, all of it connects—all of his
children, all his churches, all of his world. All are threads in a vast
tapestry of redemption. This is why a church with no global vision
is hardly a church at all. It has become disconnected. It's missing
the mind of Christ, whose passion is for every soul on this planet.

How will you respond? How will your church increase its global
vision?

Resurgent Churches are thinking about that a little more each day.

PROFILE: SCOTT AND DENISE GRINDSTAFF

The Grindstaffs are members at Grace Point and just two examples
of hearts changed forever by the global challenge. I asked Denise to
tell her own story.

There are experiences in life that can't be reduced to words. If you've stood before the Grand Canyon at sunrise, you know what I mean. A postcard just doesn't get the job done—you have to be there or you'll never get it.

Our family has had that kind of experience. For us it's been like seeing a widescreen, high-definition TV picture after a life of seeing only a small black-and-white screen. The difference is personal relationships. Let me explain.

Several years ago Scott and I had a vision of starting a coffee-house ministry for college students. We felt that was where God was leading us, and we did all the groundwork and the research. It didn't work out. We were sure, however, that God had something else for us, some kind of ministry that would help us reach people for him. More and more, we were feeling a deep desire to meet people from other countries and cultures, especially as we heard about it at Grace Point Church. Again the details never seemed to fall into line.

Grace Point had a passion for West Africa, and we began to look into short-term mission trips that would take us there. Needless to say, we instantly loved the people we met. It was a good experience, but we couldn't connect it to our vision of reaching international students at home.

Here's the part where words won't do the job. I can describe our actions—taking meals to an international student group on campus; inviting students over for dinner on Christmas Eve. But what I can't explain is how God was working. Somehow, the dinners became more frequent. Our guests became genuine friends, and our lives intertwined. "Mission activities" simply became who we were, what we did—black-and-white to full-color HD widescreen.

I could also give you numbers: more than eighty people have been in our home, with connections in twenty or more countries.

But numbers don't tell us much about souls, do they? We've been involved in weddings, in welcoming ten babies into this world. Suddenly I find my family can't be confined to a small group of photos in my wallet. It's huge! It's global. And it's something that can only be explained by the love and the power of God.

We wanted to share a few cups of coffee. A few dinners. A few smiles. What we've ended up sharing is life, measured more in hugs, daily texts, prayers, and all the little things that connect people who truly care about one another. And we know more than ever how much God cares about *us*.

CAN THESE DRY BONES LIVE?

And he said to me, "Son of man, can these bones live?"
And I answered, "O Lord GOD, you know." Then he
said to me, "Prophesy over these bones, and say to them,
O dry bones, hear the word of the LORD. Thus says the
Lord GOD to these bones: Behold, I will cause breath
to enter you, and you shall live. And I will lay sinews
upon you, and will cause flesh to come upon you, and
cover you with skin, and put breath in you, and you
shall live, and you shall know that I am the LORD."

EZEKIEL 37:3–6

EZEKIEL THE PROPHET HAD A VISION, AS HE WAS PRONE TO DO. IN IT, he walked through a weird and desolate landscape—clearly the aftermath of a terrible conflict. He had come to the valley of the shadow of death.

The prophet's imagination must have conjured the impressive battle-clad soldiers who once contended over this ground. He must have heard the clamor, the shouting, and the clanging of sword and shield. Now it was all so many bleached bones, vanishing into the shifting sands of passing time, with a deathly, ponderous silence lying heavy on the horizon.

God asked him the same question he asks us: "Can these bones live?" Can powerful, lively community emerge once again from the dust of death?

Plain reason would say no. It's not the nature of things. This army's time has passed. Life is but a vapor—even your Word says that.

God says, "You speak to them. You give them my Word. And I will give them breath. I will give flesh and muscle and life, and you'll know once again who I am."

Resurgent is a wonderful, hopeful word chosen carefully for this book. It comes from a Latin phrase that means "to rise again." Who better than a follower of Christ appreciates the idea of rising again? Everything in our faith is about new life, about triumph over death, about resurrection. Our faith is, in essence, a story of dry bones restored to life. That's good news for the wandering souls of a lost world, and it's also good news for the struggling remnants of a confused church.

God says, "You speak to them. You give them my Word. I'll provide the resurgence."

But there's actually a parallel meaning of this word *resurgence* from a separate source. Our word *surgery* is a cousin of the word *resurgence,* not a sibling. The idea of surgery, by way of Anglo-French derivation, comes from an entirely separate Latin phrase meaning "to work by hand." Which, of course, is just what surgeons do.

I like that. I like that a lot, because it suggests the work we have before us in the community. God provides the resurgence as our obedient and skilled hands provide the surgery, the loving, careful work to bring health to church and community and world.

There is so much to do and on so many levels, both local and far-reaching, both within and outside the church walls. But there is always the presence of God, always the assurance of supernatural power, always the heart of the gospel, which is incarnation and then sacrifice and then resurrection resurgence and victory.

This is not a mere head-to-head conversation, debate, or battle with the world, not a mere polite (or heated) dialogue. This is hand-to-heart, winning relationships through work. It is the hard but necessary work of earning the right to be heard. The battle rages everywhere, but the front lines are that holy ground where our presence touches the need, where believers meet skeptics, and where, in the heart of crisis, all surgeons find welcome and trust.

It begins on the day we begin to think of our community in friendship terms rather than marketing terms or even adversarial ones. It grows as we schedule a few less potluck dinners and a few more excursions to the places where the hurting lie. It deepens as we see our own people changing their future plans and giving themselves to the daily disciplines of reaching and caring; when we find them giving themselves to training in the fine arts of relational surgery.

None of this is easy. None of this can be purchased or calendared or mastered in a weekend seminar. But it can be done. It's being done within the Resurgent Church movement. Can these dry bones live again?

Notice that it's not a question we ask God. In the text, it's a question he asks us. His power stands in readiness, just as it always does. His power *surges*. It is we who need resurgence.

The question is, what are we going to do about it?

RESURGENT NETWORKS

THE NETWORKS LISTED BELOW ARE DYNAMIC AND FLUID, IN KEEPING with the culture of change we're living in. By the time you read this, a true list might be different. Many networks and/or denominations below are seeking to imagine the future and prepare today's church for its challenges. No attempt is made here to theologically brand a group over or against another. Nor are particular networks endorsed. *Caveat emptor!* Let the networker beware!

EQUIPPING

Antioch School—http://antiochschool.edu
BILD International—http://bild.org
Church Multiplication Training Center—http://cmtcmultiply.org
Church Planters—www.churchplanters.com
Creative Pastors—http://creativepastors.com
Fresh Expressions—http://freshexpressionsus.org
Gateway Leaders—http://www.gatewayleaders.com
Gospel Coalition—http://www.thegospelcoalition.org
Gospel Communities on Mission—http://www.gcmcollective.org
Hatchery—www.hatcheryla.com
Journal of Missional Practice—http://journalofmissionalpractice.com
Leadership Network—http://leadnet.org
Mike Breen—http://www.disciplingculture.com
Missio Alliance—http://www.missioalliance.org
Missional Network—http://themissionalnetwork.com
Mosaix Global Network—http://www.mosaix.info
Parish Collective—http://parishcollective.org
Passion for Planting—www.church-planting.net
Pastors.com—http://pastors.com
Plant Midwest—http://www.plantmidwest.com

Release Initiative—http://releaseinitiative.com
The Resurgent Church—www.mikemcdaniel.org
Sojourn Network—http://www.sojournnetwork.com
Willow Creek Association—http://www.willowcreek.com
Wired Churches—http://wiredchurches.com

MOBILIZATION

3DMovements—http://3dmovements.com
Assembly of God—www.churchmultiplication.net
City Church Network—http://citychur.ch
Forge America—http://www.forgeamerica.com
General Baptist: Go Project—www.goproject.us
Glocal.net—http://www.glocal.net
Missio—http://www.missio.us
Multiply Group—http://www.multiplygroup.org
Soma Tacoma—http://www.somatacoma.org
Southern Baptist: International Mission Board—www.imb.org
Southern Baptist: North American Mission Board—www.namb.net
Stadia—www.stadia.cc
United Methodist: Discipleship Ministries—www.umcdiscipleship.org
   /new-church-starts

MULTIPLICATION

9Marks—http://9marks.org
Acts 29—http://www.acts29network.org
Arch Ministries—https://archmin.org
Ecclesia—http://ecclesianet.org
Exponential—http://www.exponential.org
Fellowship Associates—http://www.fellowshipassociates.org
Missional Church Network—http://missionalchurchnetwork.com
New Thing—http://www.newthing.org
Rebuild Initiative—http://rebuildnetwork.org
Summit Network—http://www.thesummitnetwork.com
V3 Church Planting Movement—http://thev3movement.org
Verge—http://www.vergenetwork.org

CONNECTION

Convergence—www.convergenceus.org
Mesa Friends—http://mesa-friends.org
North Point Ministries—http://northpointpartners.org
Progressive Renewal—http://progressiverenewal.org

NOTES

INTRODUCTION

1. See "America's Changing Religious Landscape," Pew Research Center, http://www.pewforum.org/2015/05/12/americas-changing-religious -landscape, accessed August 20, 2015.
2. George Barna and David Kinnaman, *Churchless: Understanding Today's Unchurched and How to Connect with Them* (Carol Stream, IL: Tyndale House, 2014), 6.

CHAPTER 1

1. George Barna, *Transforming Children into Spiritual Champions: Why Children Should Be Your Church's #1 Priority* (Ventura, CA: Regal Books, 2003), 37.
2. David Kinnaman and Gabe Lyons, *Unchristian: What a New Generation Really Thinks About Christianity* (Grand Rapids: Zondervan, 2007), 18.
3. David T. Olson, *The American Church in Crisis: Groundbreaking Research Based on a National Database of Over 200,000 Churches* (Grand Rapids: Zondervan, 2008), 28.
4. Alan Hirsch, *The Forgotten Ways: Reactivating the Missional Church* (Grand Rapids: Brazos Press, 2006), 68.
5. Barna and Kinnaman, *Churchless*, 20.
6. Ed Stetzer, *Planting Churches in a Postmodern Age* (Nashville: Broadman and Holman, 2003), 7.
7. Olson, *The American Church in Crisis*, 146.

CHAPTER 2

1. Cited by Kaley Payne and Karen Mudge, "Weddings on the Increase, But Not in Churches," Bible Society, October 18, 2012, http://www.biblesociety

.org.au/news/weddings-on-the-increase-but-not-in-churches, accessed January 25, 2015.

2. Emma Green, "The Spiritual Significance of a Traditional Church Wedding," *The Atlantic*, July 25, 2014, http://www.theatlantic.com /national/archive/2014/07/how-important-is-it-to-have-a-church-wedding /374767, accessed January 25, 2015.

3. Alan Roxburgh, *The Missionary Congregation, Leadership, and Liminality* (Harrisburg, PA: Trinity Press International, 1997), 24.

4. Hirsch, *The Forgotten Ways*, 232.

5. Quoted in Ron Martoia, *Morph!: The Texture of Leadership for Tomorrow's Church*, (Loveland, CO: Group Publishing, 2003), 22.

6. Stuart Murray, *Church After Christendom* (Waynesboro, GA: Paternoster Press, 2005), 73.

7. Eddie Gibbs, *Church Morph: How Megatrends Are Reshaping Christian Communities* (Grand Rapids: Baker Books, 2009), 148–51.

8. Sarah Pulliam Bailey, "Germany's 'Cold Religion,'" *Christianity Today*, November 9, 2009.

9. Eddie Gibbs, *Rebirth of the Church: Applying Paul's Vision for Ministry in Our Post-Christian World* (Grand Rapids: Baker Academic, 2013), 25.

CHAPTER 3

1. Michael Spencer, *Mere Churchianity: Finding Your Way Back to Jesus-Shaped Spirituality* (Colorado Springs: WaterBrook, 2010), 91.

2. Millard Erickson, *Christian Theology* (Grand Rapids: Baker Academic, 1985), 770.

3. E. Stanley Jones Foundation, "The Indian Heritage and Theological Foundation of the Christian Ashram," http://www.estanleyjonesfoundation .com/wp-content/uploads/2012/03/2015-Ashram-Movement-for-the-History -project.pdf, accessed August 20, 2015.

4. Stanley J. Grenz, *A Primer on Postmodernism* (Grand Rapids: Eerdmans, 1996), 169.

5. Quoted in Gibbs, *Rebirth of the Church*, 65.

6. Dietrich Bonhoeffer, *God Is in the Manger: Reflections on Advent and Christmas*, ed. Jana Reiss, trans. O. C. Dean Jr. (Louisville: Westminster John Knox Press, 2010), 22.

7. Josh Kelley, *Radically Normal* (Eugene, OR: Harvest House, 2014).

CHAPTER 4

1. Gregory Benford, "The Future That Never Was: Pictures from the Past," *Popular Mechanics*, January 27, 2011, http://www.popularmechanics.com/flight/g462 /future-that-never-was-next-gen-tech-concepts, accessed June 16, 2015.

2. Clifford Stoll, "Why the Web Won't Be Nirvana," *Newsweek*, February 26,

1995, http://www.newsweek.com/clifford-stoll-why-web-wont-be-nirvana -185306, accessed June 16, 2015.

3. Roxburgh, *The Missionary Congregation, Leadership, and Liminality*, 13.

4. Kim A. Lawton, "Outreach: Evangelism Explosion Retools Its Approach," *Christianity Today*, March 3, 1997, http://www.christianitytoday.com/ct /1997/march3/7t3058.html, accessed June 15, 2015.

5. Thomas L. Friedman, *The World Is Flat: A Brief History of the Twenty-First Century* (New York: Farrar, Straus and Giroux, 2006).

6. See Marshall McLuhan, *The Gutenberg Galaxy: The Making of Typographic Man* (Toronto: University of Toronto Press, 1962) and *Understanding Media: The Extensions of Man* (New York: McGraw-Hill, 1964).

7. Robert Wuthnow, *Boundless Faith: The Global Outreach of American Churches* (Berkeley and Los Angeles: University of California Press, 2009), 1.

8. Ibid.

9. D'Vera Cohn, "Multi-Race and the 2010 Census," Pew Research Center, April 6, 2011, http://www.pewresearch.org/2011/04/06/multirace-and-the -2010-census, accessed June 25, 2015.

10. David Swanson, "Down with the Homogeneous Unit Principle," *Christianity Today*, August 2, 2010, http://www.christianitytoday.com/le /2010/august-online-only/down-with-homogeneous-unit-principle.html, accessed June 25, 2015.

11. George Gallup Jr. and Timothy Jones, *The Next American Spirituality: Finding God in the Twenty-First Century* (Colorado Springs: Cook Communications, 2000), 49.

12. Michael Kress, "The Kabbalah craze: Stars embrace mystic beliefs, and many rabbinical scholars cringe," Religion News Blog, July 24, 2004. http://www.religionnewsblog.com/7988/the-kabbalah-craze

13. Robert Webber, *Ancient-Future Faith: Rethinking Evangelicalism for a Postmodern World* (Grand Rapids: Baker, 1999), 27.

14. Mark Yaconelli, quoted in Tony Jones, *Postmodern Youth Ministry* (Grand Rapids: Zondervan, 2006), 90.

CHAPTER 5

1. Elizabeth Gilbert, *Eat, Pray, Love: One Woman's Search for Everything Across Italy, India and Indonesia* (New York: Viking, 2006).

2. Ross Douthat, *Bad Religion: How We Became a Nation of Heretics* (New York: Free Press, 2012).

3. Ibid., 215–16.

4. Cited in Eddie Gibbs, *ChurchNext: Quantum Changes in How We Do Ministry* (Downers Grove, IL: InterVarsity, 2000), 72.

5. Glenn T. Stanton, "FactChecker: Misquoting Francis of Assisi", July 10, 2012, http://www.thegospelcoalition.org/article/factchecker-misquoting -francis-of-assisi, accessed June 30, 2015.

6. See George Hunsberger, "The Newbigin Gauntlet: Developing a Domestic Missiology for North America," in *The Church Between Gospel and Culture*, ed. George R. Hunsberger and Craig Van Gelder (Grand Rapids: Eerdmans, 1996), 6.
7. Brian McLaren was a lecturer in one of the author's doctrinal seminars, and throughout the week he advocated the idea of new doctrines.
8. George Barna, *Evangelism That Works: How to Reach Changing Generations with the Unchanging Gospel* (Ventura, CA: Regal, 1995), 36.
9. John Stott, *The Contemporary Christian: Applying God's Word to Today's World* (Downers Grove, IL: InterVarsity, 1992), 358.

CHAPTER 6

1. Gibbs, *Rebirth of the Church*, 59.
2. Timothy Keller, *Center Church: Doing Balanced, Gospel-Centered Ministry in Your City* (Grand Rapids: Zondervan, 2012), 173.
3. Charles Kraft, *Christianity in Culture: A Study in Biblical Theologizing in Cross-Cultural Perspective* (Maryknoll, NY: Orbis, 2005).
4. Ibid., 247–49.
5. Gerardo Marti, *A Mosaic of Believers: Diversity and Innovation in a Multiethnic Church* (Bloomington: Indiana University Press, 2005), 56.

CHAPTER 7

1. Mark Galli, "Learning to Count to One: New Math for Those Addicted to Getting Higher and Highers in Their Churches," *Christianity Today*, February 17, 2011, http://www.christianitytoday.com/ct/2011/februaryweb-only/learningcountone.html?start=1, accessed August 22, 2015.
2. Marty King, "Number of SBC Churches Increased Last Year; Members, Attendance, and Baptisms Declined," Lifeway, June 6, 2013, http://www.lifeway.com/Article/news-2012-southern-baptist-annual-church-profile-report, accessed August 26, 2013.
3. Reggie McNeal, *Missional Renaissance: Changing the Scorecard for the Church* (San Francisco: Jossey-Bass, 2009), 111–27.
4. Interview with author, March 15, 2015.
5. Erwin McManus, *An Unstoppable Force: Daring to Become the Church God Had in Mind*, 2nd ed. (Colorado Springs: David C. Cook, 2013), 18.

CHAPTER 8

1. Sherry Turkle, *Alone Together: Why We Expect More from Technology and Less from Each Other* (New York: Basic Books, 2011).
2. Sherry Turkle, "The Flight from Conversation," *New York Times Sunday*

Review, April 21, 2012, http://www.nytimes.com/2012/04/22/opinion/
sunday/the-flight-from-conversation.html?_r=0..

3. Nicholas A. Christakis and James H. Fowler, *Connected: The Surprising Power of Our Social Networks and How They Shape Our Lives* (New York: Little, Brown, 2009), 18.

4. Ibid., 67.

5. Craig Detweiler, *iGods: How Technology Shapes Our Spiritual and Social Lives* (Grand Rapids: Brazos Press, 2013), 163.

6. Jacques Ellul, *The Humiliation of the Word*, trans. Joyce Main Hanks (Grand Rapids: Eerdmans, 1985).

7. Detweiler, *iGods*, 234.

8. Eugene Peterson, *A Long Slow Obedience in the Same Direction: Discipleship in an Instant Society* (Downers Grove, IL: InterVarsity, 1980).

9. Read Mercer Schuchardt, "Taming the Image," *Christianity Today*, Spring 2011, http://www.christianitytoday.com/le/2011/spring/tamingimage. html?paging=off, accessed September 18, 2015.

10. Linda Stone coined this phrase in her article "Continuous Partial Attention—Not the Same as Multi-Tasking," Bloomberg Business, July 24, 2008, http://www.businessweek.com/business_at_work/time_management /archives/2008/07/continuous_part.html, accessed August 1, 2015.

11. Slices, "We Get Most of Our News from Facebook Now," *Relevant* magazine (September–October 2015): 20.

12. Detweiler, *iGods*, 229.

13. Erwin McManus, *The Artisan Soul: Crafting Your Life into a Work of Art* (San Francisco: HarperOne, 2014).

14. "What We Believe," Soma Tacoma, n.d., http://www.somatacoma.org /what-we-believe, accessed April 14, 2015.

15. Hirsch, *The Forgotten Ways*, 222.

16. Stephen E. Ambrose, *Band of Brothers: E Company, 506th Regiment, 101st Airborne: From Normandy to Hitler's Eagle's Nest* (New York: Simon & Schuster, 1992); Erik Jendresen et al., *Band of Brothers*, directed by Phil Alden Robinson et al., 10 episodes (New York: Home Box Office, 2001).

CHAPTER 9

1. Stephen Mansfield, "The Story of God and Guinness," *Relevant*, March 24, 2010, http://www.relevantmagazine.com/god/mission/features/20993-god -and-guinness, accessed September 6, 2015.

2. Alan Hirsch, *The Forgotten Ways: Reactivating the Missional Church* (Grand Rapids: Brazos Press, 2006), 18.

3. Tom Rath, *Strengths Finder 2.0* (New York: Gallup Press, 2007), 105.

4. Erwin McManus, *The Barbarian Way: Unleash the Untamed Faith Within* (Nashville: Thomas Nelson, 2005), 64.

5. Everett M. Rogers, *Diffusion of Innovations*, 5th ed. (New York: Free Press, 2003), 281.
6. Emily McFarlan Miller, "4 Churches Changing Everything," *Relevant* (May–June 2015): 44–45, http://www.relevantmagazine.com/god/church/4-churches-changing-everything.

CHAPTER 10

1. Tim Stafford, "Go and Plant Churches of All Peoples," *Christianity Today*, September 27, 2007, http://www.christianitytoday.com/ct/2007/september/36.68.html, 69.
2. C. Peter Wagner, *Church Planting for a Greater Harvest: A Comprehensive Guide* (Ventura, CA: Regal, 1990), 11.
3. Peter Kendrick, email interview with the author, May 7, 2009. Within the Southern Baptist Convention, 15.6 percent in 2003 and 15.5 percent in 2005 gave birth to sister churches. Involvement varied from primary sponsorship, clustering, sponsorship, or supporting sponsorship.
4. Geoff Surratt, "Why in the world would you attend Exponential?" Exponential, n.d., https://www.exponential.org/why-in-the-world-would-you-attend-exponential, accessed September 8, 2015.
5. North American Mission Board, "Multi-Site Church Planting," n.d., http://www.namb.net/namb1cb1col.aspx?id=8590001111, accessed September 9, 2015.
6. Warren Bird and Kristen Walters, *Multisite Is Multiplying: Survey Identifies Leading Practices and Confirms New Developments in the Movement's Expansion* (Dallas: Leadership Network, 2010), 2–3.
7. Geoff Surratt, Greg Ligon, and Warren Bird, *The Multi-Site Church Revolution: Being One Church—In Many Locations* (Grand Rapids: Zondervan, 2006), 21. The following are the seven churches in the top ten that had multisites: Without Walls International, Tampa, Florida; Mount Zion Baptist Church, White Creeks, Tennessee; LifeChurch.tv, Oklahoma City, Oklahoma; Saddleback Community Church, Lake Forest, California; The Fountain of Praise, Houston, Texas; Second Baptist Church, Houston, Texas; and Franklin Avenue Baptist Church, New Orleans, Louisiana.

CHAPTER 11

1. Quoted in Gunther Gassmann and Scott Hendrix, *Fortress Introduction to the Luther Confessions* (Minneapolis: Fortress, 1999), 12.
2. Center for the Study of Global Christianity, "Status of Global Mission, 2014, in the Context of AD 1800–2025," January 2014, http://www.gordonconwell.edu/resources/documents/StatusOfGlobalMission.pdf, accessed September 15, 2015.
3. Morgan Lee, "Leaving Baptist in Your Church Name Won't Scare People Away," *Christianity Today*, June 3, 2015, http://www.christianitytoday

.com/gleanings/2015/june/leaving-baptist-in-your-church-name-wont -scare-people-away.html, accessed September 10, 2015.

4. Jeremy Weber, "Should Your Church's Name Include Its Denomination?" *Christianity Today*, February 22, 2013, http://www.christianitytoday .com/gleanings/2013/february/should-your-churchs-name-include-its -denomination.html, accessed September 10, 2015.

5. Albert Mohler, "A Call for Theological Triage and Christian Maturity," May 20, 2004, http://www.albertmohler.com/2004/05/20 /a-call-for-theological-triage-and-christian-maturity-2, accessed September 14, 2015.

6. Gibbs, *Church Morph*, 23.

7. Bob Roberts Jr., *Glocalizaton: How Followers of Jesus Engage the New Flat World* (Grand Rapids: Zondervan, 2007), 171.

8. Will Mancini, *Church Unique: How Missional Leaders Cast Vision, Capture Culture, and Create Movement* (San Francisco: Jossey-Bass, 2008), 15–16.

9. Seth Godin, *Tribes: We Need You to Lead Us* (New York: Portfolio, 2008), 5.

10. J. D. Greear, "Not Just Seating Capacity but Sending Capacity," Send Network, April 4, 2014, http://sendnetwork.com/2014/04/04/seating -capacity-sending-capacity, accessed September 15, 2015.

CHAPTER 12

1. Paul Borthwick, *How to Be a World-Class Christian: Becoming Part of God's Global Kingdom*, rev. ed. (Downers Grove, IL: InterVarsity, 2010), 46–47.

2. Center for the Study of Global Christianity, *Christianity in Its Global Context, 1970–2020: Society, Religion, and Mission* (South Hamilton, MA: Gordon-Conwell Theological Seminary, 2013), http://wwwgordonconwell. com/netcommunity/CSGCResources/ChristianityinitsGlobalContext.pdf, 76, accessed September 16, 2015.

3. Bob Smietana, "The Southern Baptist S(p)ending Crunch," *Christianity Today*, November 2015, 65.

4. Henry Blackaby and Richard Blackaby, *Experiencing God: Knowing and Doing the Will of God*, rev. ed. (Nashville: Lifeway, 2008), 184.

5. Fritz Kling, *The Meeting of the Waters: 7 Global Currents That Will Propel the Future Church* (Colorado Springs: David C. Cook, 2010), 102.

6. McManus, *The Barbarian Way*, 103.

7. "Friendship Evangelism," Ethnic Harvest, n.d., http://www .ethnicharvest.org/ideas/friendship.htm, accessed September 28, 2015.

ABOUT THE AUTHOR

 **MIKE MCDANIEL** IS THE FOUNDING PASTOR OF Grace Point Church in Northwest Arkansas. A native of the area, Mike, his wife, Lori, and their three children launched this purposeful, intentional church. Since its successful launch they have planted multiple other churches in the area and around the world.

Before starting the church in Arkansas, Mike and his family served as church developers with the International Mission Board (IMB) in the Republic of Zambia, South Africa. He has a doctoral degree from Dallas Theological Seminary, as well as degrees from Mid-America Baptist Seminary and Southwest Baptist University. McDaniel is also a CrossFit Level 1 Certified Trainer.

www.TheResurgent.Church

ALSO AVAILABLE FROM
NEXT
LEADERSHIP NETWORK
WHEREVER BOOKS ARE SOLD

ISBN: 9780718032883
ISBN: 9780718032890 (E-BOOK)

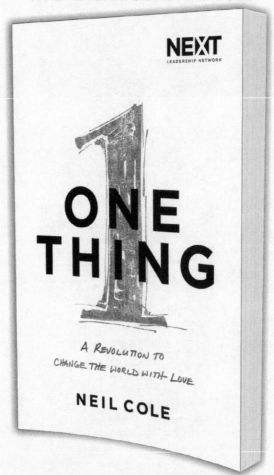